Voluntary Work and the Environment:

Local Environmental Development Initiatives in Europe

EF/92/09/EN

European Foundation
for the Improvement of
Living and Working Conditions

Voluntary Work and the Environment:

Local Environmental Development Initiatives in Europe

by
Dr. Nicholas Falk

Loughlinstown House, Shankill, Co. Dublin, Ireland
Tel: 282 68 88 Fax: 282 64 56 Telex: 30726 EURF EI

Cataloguing data can be found at the end of this publication

Luxembourg: Office for Official Publications of the European Communities, 1992

ISBN 92-826-3650-X

Printed in Ireland

PREFACE

The growing awareness of the importance and potential of voluntary work in several Member States as a supplement to various public services, as well as the growing environmental awareness in society, led the Foundation to introduce a new theme into its four-year programme 1985-1988 under the heading "Initiatives linked to Voluntary Work in the Environment".

In 1985, studies were commissioned in Belgium, the Federal Republic of Germany, France, Italy, the Netherlands and the United Kingdom, and the researchers were asked to focus on voluntary work in relation to local initiatives in the environment. Such initiatives appeared to be developing most rapidly, but little was known about them. It was also agreed that special attention be paid to voluntary work aimed at improving and protecting the environment in and around urban centres, thus linking the studies with the Foundation's other activities on living conditions in these areas. Finally, it was decided that only those initiatives which would usually not be undertaken as part of a contract involving paid activity be investigated.

The six studies were completed in 1986 and have been published in the Foundation's working paper series. They showed, as was expected, that, despite some similarities, the nature, scope and organization of and the traditions relating to voluntary work in the environment often differ considerably from one Member State to the other. This situation is reflected, for instance, in the diversity of cases and areas dealt with in the national reports.

The Foundation also commissioned Dr. Nicholas Falk of the Urban and Economic Development Group (URBED), London, to draw up a report based on the findings of the six national studies as well as his own and extensive experience from many years involvement in voluntary activities. This report was amended in the light of discussions with the researchers in charge of the national studies and the representative of the Foundation, and it was later revised, updated and enlarged.

The present publication is not a typical consolidated research report synthesizing, analyzing and comparing the findings of the national studies. In fact, the very different national traditions in this rather unstructured area did not lend themselves to such a rigid comparative exercise. Because of the subject, it was also considered important that the report be aimed at a wide audience and that it, therefore, should provide an easily accessible and well written account of the various types of local environmental voluntary action, their characteristics, scope, role, potential and limits as well as the problems they were facing. Hence, the author has chosen to present and discuss the issues more generally, using an informal and personal approach and style and drawing upon his own experience and the national reports to explain and illustrate his statements. In doing so, it was difficult to avoid the report, to some extent, reflecting the views of the author rather than those of some of the researchers involved in the national studies.

A meeting was held in Brussels, on 7 October 1987, to enable representatives of the employers, trades unions, governments and the Commission of the European Commission - the constituent bodies of the Foundation's Administrative Board - to evaluate the findings of this report. The participants underlined that voluntary action might have a considerable potential in our society in view of the major and ongoing economic, social, cultural and demographic changes. Voluntary work in the environment should, however, be part of or coordinated with the general efforts and planning of the public authorities in this area, although in a way which allowed sufficient scope for flexibility and creativity. Furthermore, public authorities should establish a formalised structure for this type of activity in order to ensure the safety of the people involved and the effectiveness and continuity of the work. They should, for instance, insure the volunteers against accidents and should provide the guidance, equipment and materials required. It was also considered important that voluntary work should not, in any way, be used as a means of releasing public authorities from their responsibilities towards society, particularly in areas like the environment. Such work should, on the contrary, supplement the programmes and actions of public authorities and it should never be used for creating unpaid jobs or, otherwise, for substituting paid work, whether permanent or temporary. Finally, the participants suggested that the scope of the European Heritage Fund be enlarged to comprise also projects relating to the industrial heritage with a European perspective, and that contributions to voluntary work in the environment be made tax deductible in the same way as those made for cultural purposes and charity. Such a system should then be combined with the creation of national funds distributing the contributions to relevant projects in this area.

Following this meeting and further discussions, the present report was updated, revised and enlarged in 1990.

Jørn Pedersen
Dublin, March 1992

SUMMARY

VOLUNTARY WORK AND THE ENVIRONMENT:
Local environmental development initiatives in Europe

This report was commissioned by the European Foundation for the Improvement of Living and Working Conditions to examine a number of issues, including:

- what is voluntary work?
- how can volunteers improve the environment?
- what impact do they have on paid employment?
- where is voluntary work appropriate?
- how should it be strengthened?

The report is based on studies in six countries (Belgium, France, Germany, Italy, the Netherlands and the United Kingdom). In each country, researchers consulted the literature, carried out surveys and interviews, talked to experts, and selected and wrote up between 6 and 12 small case studies of projects that were considered exemplary. The research team met three times to ensure a common approach and to compare findings.

The main conclusions are summarised below. The first important point is that the term voluntary work means many different things. It is officially defined as work that is not obligatory, but is socially relevant, unpaid and carried out with some degree of organisation. There is, however, a great difference between national voluntary organisations motivated by philanthropy, and local initiatives motivated by community action or a spirit of mutual aid. There are also a growing number of voluntary initiatives that aim to be community businesses or development trusts, and provide permanent employment. There are also in most countries a number of agencies providing technical aid. Together these potentially add up to a 'third force' that can bridge the gap between the public and the private sectors.

Voluntary sector projects are improving the environment in three main areas. First, they are tackling the problems of urban sprawl and dereliction by improving open spaces. Second, they are helping maintain the heritage of historic buildings and monuments by restoring the built environment. Finally, and in a smaller number of cases, they are trying to improve the quality of life by conserving natural resources.

The roles of voluntary groups vary, but there is a common progression that takes place. Initiatives often start with individuals protesting about a threat. They then form groups which mobilise volunteers and who serve as missionaries or pioneers in showing what is possible. They also act as promoters or animateurs in areas that have lost activity, often drawing on labour from government schemes for the unemployed. Some groups go on to act as environmental managers or even developers, in order to generate independent sources of finance to sustain their activities.

Voluntary work generally complements and enhances paid employment. Benefits include better job satisfaction, temporary jobs for the unemployed, preparation of the young for employment, and some new kinds of work, particularly in environmental management and through business spin-offs. Generally, there is no threat to permanent jobs, provided government support is local initiatives, concentrated on development and training as opposed to maintenance work.

Voluntary work is most appropriate when it responds to new needs, and involves the community in local initiatives. The strengths, which continually lead to the birth of new groups, include community involvement and therefore relevance, multiple benefits from complex projects, a capacity to innovate, low overheads, the scope for involving the disadvantaged, commitment, and the maintenance of freedom of expression or democracy. The weaknesses, which cause many groups to collapse, include vulnerability and over-dependence on charismatic leaders, unrealistic objectives, fragmentation and isolation, and a tendency towards amateurishness.

Where projects have been particularly successful, a number of key factors for success can be identified. These include:

- starting with the right driving force (or social
  entrepreneur)
- forging partnerships between the community and authority
- tapping professional expertise
- showing early results
- having some fun
- exploiting the media
- spreading the administrative load

The increasing environmental awareness in Europe provides an excellent basis for taking steps in all the member countries to strengthen the role ordinary people can play in improving their environment. A series of ideas are put forward in the report aimed at increasing recognition, opening up additional sources of funds, and providing technical aid. The most important proposal is to extend the European Heritage Fund to cover major projects involving the industrial heritage, and to provide tax incentives to enable local initiatives to diversify their funding base.

Other suggestions for consideration by the EC and national governments are to make what might be called Local Environmental Development Initiatives more effective. A first step is to provide support for running 'networks' at the national and European levels. Consideration also needs to be given to treating development trusts as if they formed part of the public sector, so that they can obtain grants from the EC direct.

There is also a need in some countries to provide legal protection and insurance cover on reasonable terms.

A number of proposals are put forward to expand funding for well-run projects. These include identifying voluntary projects as demonstration projects within EC Integrated Operations Programmes, and funding the feasibility studies that are needed to package finance from different sources. Governments should fund designated posts concerned with the management of volunteers and those on temporary employment schemes.

There is also a need for medium-term service contracts to enable voluntary groups to 'sell' their services to public authorities. An investigation is needed into ways of linking public grants for heritage projects with private tax incentives to make local initiatives less dependent on government funding.

Finally, some practical suggestions are put forward for expanding technical aid to promising local initiatives, through European travel fellowships, public support for community technical aid centres, and more funding earmarked for training in project management skills. The aim is to enable groups that have established themselves to attain a degree of self-sufficiency and to employ staff who would otherwise be unemployed. This will involve encouraging the growth of community businesses and development trusts.

CONTENTS

1 THE AIMS AND APPROACH OF THE STUDY

2 Aims of the research

The European Foundation's study on voluntary work in the environment covers six Member States: Belgium, France, Germany, Italy, the Netherlands and the United Kingdom. It is based on a review of the changing scene in each country, and a series of between 6 and 12 short case studies focusing on some of the more significant local initiatives.

The aim of this study was to contribute to:

o   establishing a European picture of the potential, the characteristics, the organisation, the problems and the national differences and similarities in relation to this type of work

o   improving the urban environment and other parts of the environment affecting the urban population

o   illustrating to what extent this form of activity may be a means of creating permanent jobs

o   providing meaningful activities for certain categories of the population looking for a more active life, e.g. the unemployed, the early retired, some categories of young people

o exchanging information on experience, whether positive or negative, and on
   specific activities relating to such initiatives, which may be of interest to other
   Member States, thereby also learning about possible improvements regarding
   voluntary work as an important element of the above-mentioned efforts

o providing the European Community institutions with information which may
   assist them in defining their role and interest in this area and the steps to be
   taken in support of initiatives of particular relevance to Community policies

2.1 Voluntary work and its background

There is clearly a connection between this study and the changing nature of the European industrial economy, and the stresses which are being created, particularly in the older urban areas. Three main problems can be distinguished. First is the **growing amount of leisure time,** with shorter working hours and as people retire earlier or take longer to find paid work. Work gives a meaning and structure to life, and creates opportunities for making friends, as well as providing an income. Finding something satisfying to do in company with other people will continue to be a challenge even if unemployment were to fall. There is also the problem of compensating for the sterility and lack of satisfaction associated with many of today's jobs, where people may be cut off from both nature and a sense of producing something of value. This study therefore addresses the issue of creating worthwhile work in a post-industrial society.

Second, there is the problem of **improving the quality of the environment**. This is particularly important in decaying urban areas that have lost their traditional industrial functions, leaving behind empty buildings and wasteland. Local authorities may lack either the resources or the means of promoting the regeneration of such areas. They also face the problem of stirring people into action and developing a sense of civic pride. At the same time cities are sprawling, and there are pressures on both the countryside and traditional villages. The quality of the environment is also under threat in many places as a result of pollution, while natural resources are being used up at a prodigious rate. This study therefore also deals with the issue of how to encourage environmental initiatives.

The third problem is that **tension and conflicts** can be caused when people live in close proximity to each other, and when their neighbourhood begins visibly to decline. At the very least it encourages those who are most able to leave, and at worst it can promote vandalism, riots and the abandonment of property. At the same time, people may feel increasingly alienated and isolated, as traditional institutions like the family or conventional employment break down. This sense of 'Future Shock', as Alvin Toffler calls it, may require new forms of associations to harness people's energy in creative rather than destructive directions. Hence this study is also concerned with the organisation of society.

Nobody would argue that 'voluntary work' is the answer to all the negative forces that prevail, and some think it could divert attention from finding the real solutions. More and more people, however, including politicians of different attitudes, have realised that voluntary action is an important and under-utilised resource that can be harnessed to promote individual and community regeneration. This message comes out clearly from all the national reports commissioned for this study. Indeed, some have gone so far as to suggest that voluntary action forms a 'third force', combining the benevolent aspects of the public sector with the entrepreneurial aspects of the private sector (a concept that emerged in the USA in the 1970s). More recently some thinkers, particularly in France, have begun to define a new area of activity, the 'social economy', which might in time grow to become an important 'industry' like mining or tourism.

The growth of voluntary action as a force can in part be explained by changes in attitudes towards volunteering. The roots of voluntary action lie in **philanthropy** and was originally mainly associated with the social services, e.g. caring for the elderly and the poor. It was also, in some cases, a response to emergencies, like the life boat service in the UK. Research shows that there is a general interest among volunteers in feeling useful and meeting other people with similar interests. However, volunteers in the environmental field tend to have rather more complex motives and, according to a British survey, tend to be much more idealistic than the average volunteer.

A very different motive underlies what is called **community action,** that is where groups of people come together to fight to improve their conditions. Often the motivating force is one of resisting a threat, such as a motorway, or protesting about some common problem, like poorly built housing. The essential philosophy is that of 'mutual aid'. However, such groups sometimes go on to tackle practical projects in order to maintain the support of their members and to achieve results quickly. Collective action of this kind is undoubtedly important in developing organisational as well as technical skills. It can also help to boost local pride and strengthen the group's image, both of which are essential but difficult elements to carry out in the process of regenerating run-down areas. Many of those who would formerly have worked within political parties or written pamphlets are now driven to initiate schemes that will help to show the way, or simply be worthwhile in themselves. Others want also to apply know-how or a professional skill through projects that enable them to put their knowledge into practice. This may, for instance, be the driving force for ecologists, landscape architects and other professional groups and also those who are interested in more decentralised approaches and alternatives.

Finally there is a further kind of mixed activity, which is run as a business but in the public interest, and which provides a crucial element in the growth of voluntary action as an economic force. These are sometimes called **community businesses.** For example, in Britain and the Netherlands there is the the housing association movement. Though housing associations may be far removed from the average environmental project, their 'not for profit' status and reliance on unpaid boards of management give them common elements. Housing associations today provide some 600,000 rented houses in Britain and most of the rented housing in the Netherlands. Though most of their staff are now paid, all have their origins in voluntary effort, and are run by management councils or directors who draw no fees, but instead derive the satisfaction that they are helping society. While the precise equivalents vary throughout Europe, and for example in Italy are largely run as cooperatives, this is a significant form of activity that can also be classed as being in the voluntary sector and concerned with the environment. When all the different initiatives are combined, voluntary action can be seen as a 'third force', distinct from either the public or private sectors.

2.2 The scope for environmental initiatives

In recent years there has been a growing concern with all aspects of the environment in every European country. In part this reflects rising living standards and the increased importance placed on public spaces. It probably also reflects a desire to preserve our heritage from redevelopment or decay. This applies particularly in older inner city areas that are blighted by the spread of modern office blocks and the loss of traditional neighbourhoods such as the Marolles in Brussels (see **Appendix A** for list of case studies). There is equally a concern in many countries to conserve the habitats of wildlife, whether this involves maintaining forests better, as in Holland, protecting amphibians, as in Germany, or creating nature parks, as in England. There is also a growing concern to apply ecological principles and to conserve and hence extend the life of natural resources. These concerns are being taken up by almost all political parties and by the Commission of the European Communities.

Many of the improvements that people want involve massive shifts of resources, and can only therefore be effected by action at government level. But there also appear to be what can best be called **local initiatives** which make a significant contribution at the levels where people live and work. What is considered important and what is possible will vary from country to country and place to place, but there is a surprising similarity between case studies in the different national reports. However, within a large city, for example, creating green areas may be of much greater importance than in smaller towns where access to the countryside is easy. While the case studies show that some types of initiative are being carried out throughout Europe, it is likely that national preferences and conditions differ in the importance placed on different aspects of the environment. The English, for example, may be more interested in planting vegetation, while the Italians may be more concerned with the conservation of monuments.

The cases studied as part of this European project show that the range of action undertaken by volunteers and organisations concerned with voluntary work is very considerable, even though it may still be very fragmented and often disorganised.   A useful classification, which emerged from the project, distinguishes between three main types of activity.   The first type involves **improving open spaces**, and can range from tidying up wasteland to planting trees or introducing new uses, such as urban farms as for example at the Windmill Hill City Farm in Bristol (see **Appendix B** for summary of case study). It can also involve maintaining the wildlife that already exists, whether in forests on the edge of towns, as in Forêt de Soignes on the edge of Brussels, or amphibian life in people's back gardens, as in the German City of Dortmund (see **Appendix B**).   The second type of action involves **restoring the built environment**, which can include stopping demolition, finding new uses for old buildings, and organising and undertaking repairs.   It can involve industrial artifacts like canals or buildings from the Industrial Revolution as in the Canal du Centre project in Wallonia, Belgium. It can also include building up and maintaining cultural artifacts, as in the conservation of cave dwellings in Matera, Italy. The third type of action involves **conserving natural resources**. This can include measures to promote energy conservation or recycling materials, such as paper and other items that would have been thrown away, as in the Ecological Cycle Foundation's work in the Netherlands (see **Appendix B**). It can also involve reducing pollution. An example is the World Wide Fund for Nature's project which collects used batteries in Ravenna, Italy, to avoid acid polluting the sea. It is also possible to consider as separate types of project those primarily concerned with meeting the needs of young people, and those involving industrial archaeology or 'industrial tourism', like the project that trains some 30 retired employees of Le Creusot/Montceau-les-Mines to act as guides (see **Appendix B**). However, in general the three-fold classification is helpful in describing the main concern environmental groups tend to have.

2.3 Research approach

Because statistics on voluntary work are very limited and hard to collect, the focus of this study has been on identifying and examining interesting examples of voluntary action in the environment. The method used was to consult with environmental organisations in each country and to review the literature on voluntary action (see **Appendix C** for a short reading list). In some countries, for example Germany, a survey was circulated to groups known to be undertaking initiatives. An initial sample was then selected of around 20 projects, from which at least six projects were picked to be studied in depth. The case studies were chosen to cover a range of initiatives and also to include examples that would be of interest throughout Europe. They are considered representative of projects that have succeeded (though of course many other projects do good work without achieving as much). The case studies followed a similar structure, and involved talking to more than one person about how the project was set up, what problems it had overcome, and what help was needed. The case studies were generally prepared by consultants, including academic researchers and journalists. Interestingly in the German study the groups were commissioned to write up their own stories. The methodology and conclusions were discussed at three coordination meetings.

The main aim of the study is to establish the significance of voluntary action as a social and environmental force, both now and potentially. In particular, it considers a number of policy issues that are of current concern to both the individual Member States and the European Commission. While the national reports document experience in each of the countries, the main thrust of this report is in producing some guidance that may be useful in shaping public policy as well as sharing experience more widely. the overall concern is with predominantly urban areas, as these have suffered most from the decline of traditional employment. However, some of the examples have been drawn from further afield where there are useful lessons to be learnt from them.

2.4 Policy issues

Five main policy issues have been identified:

a) **What does voluntary work really mean?** The term 'voluntary' work is used differently in the UK and France from other Member States. It is commonly used to describe work that is essentially unpaid, as well as work that is done 'freely', that is without compulsion. But it turns out that in most other European countries the more significant voluntary organisations, those that are tackling projects involving investment in buildings for example, have some paid staff. Also, many make use of the different government 'job creation' or temporary employment and training schemes to extend their services and undertake development projects. We have therefore sought to establish whether there is a distinct 'third' sector involving voluntary effort that can be contrasted with the public or private sectors, and whether community action needs to be considered separately from other forms of voluntary action.

b) **How can volunteers improve the environment?** The environmental challenges facing the older industrial areas of Europe often seem too large and too complex for voluntary action to be relevant. There is therefore an issue of whether local, national or European governmental bodies should make any effort to support voluntary work in this field. The national studies have thus sought to establish whether there is a European-wide phenomenon, and to evaluate its potential significance in terms of creating a better environment.

c) **What impact does voluntary work have on paid employment?** With high rates of unemployment, there is concern everywhere that work undertaken by volunteers or voluntary organisations does not substitute for existing jobs, particularly those in the public sector that are covered by trade unions, or that would have otherwise been undertaken by private business. Hence, there is a widely held concern that voluntary organisations should only do work that would not otherwise have been undertaken, and that they should not receive an unfair subsidy. However, there may also be the potential within the voluntary sector to provide experiences that will lead on to permanent jobs or that will create the conditions for economic recovery. It is important to consider what kinds of people are involved in voluntary work, and whether it is largely in addition to, or instead of, regular jobs. There is also an issue relating to the role of voluntary associations in taking responsibility for job creation schemes or schemes that provide worthwhile work and training for those who are unemployed.

d) **Where is voluntary work most appropriate?** As there will be no simple answer to whether voluntary work is a 'good thing', it is important to establish the circumstances in which voluntary action is most appropriate. These might include, for example, work which does not involve unusual skills or sophisticated machinery. But they may also involve situations where people develop new skills or abilities that change their lives. Hence the case studies examine how projects 'got off the ground', including the role of what have been called 'social entrepreneurs' and the attitudes of the other actors, and the link between voluntary projects, local authorities, and the business community.

e) **How should voluntary work be organised and supported?** As effectiveness and efficiency both depend on management - that is how human and other resources are deployed and motivated - it is important to establish what forms of organisation have proved most useful in achieving results. Issues often arise out of the relationship between volunteers and paid staff, which depend on the scale of the activity (just as the management problems of a new small firm are very different from those facing an established company). The different national studies examine whether there is a general pattern of development. There are also national differences in the laws governing voluntary work which may require some form of European-wide structure or source of support. Thus it has been argued that it is vital to provide voluntary initiatives with professional technical assistance to enable them to be more effective. This can range from 'feasibility studies' to ongoing consultancy help from architects and other experts. In passing, the research has looked for ways in which technical assistance is made available and funded in the different Member States, and also considered how far it is the crucial factor in determining whether projects are successful in attaining their aims. In particular the report considers whether there is a case for sharing information and expertise at a national or European level.

2.5 Conclusions

Voluntary work traditionally grew out of philanthropy and the social services, such as the welfare of the elderly. Increasingly, however, it is motivated by a deep-seated concern to tackle the environmental and social challenges arising from the decline of our traditional cities and industries as a result of the massive technological and economic changes affecting Europe. The scope for practical local initiatives is considerable, in the fields of improving open spaces, restoring the built environment and conserving natural resources. They can also have particular relevance to meeting the needs of youth and possibly of improving run-down areas. However, before more support will be made available, there are a number of policy issues to be resolved including the meaning of voluntary work, the impact it can make on environmental problems, competition with paid work, contribution to personal development, the need for training, organisation and assistance. These issues are dealt with in the chapters that follow.

2   THE NATURE OF VOLUNTARY WORK

There is a major issue over the contribution of voluntary work and whether it is worth encouraging. Some argue that people are primarily motived by money, and that the market should determine where resources go. Others emphasise the role of the democratic processes of government in counteracting market imperfections. Such simplistic dichotomy leaves voluntary action in a kind of ideological no-mans land, where it is tolerated but not encouraged, or seen merely as a temporary stop-gap. The basic problem stems from the ambiguous nature of voluntary work and voluntary organisations, which covers not only a variety of types of work, from caring to campaigning, but also are motivated by many different objectives. Before considering the contribution voluntary work can make in the environment, it is necessary to set it in a European perspective, and then to distinguish between the different types of organisation involved.

2.1   The nature of volunteering

Pressure to stop voluntary work competing with paid work, together with the search for new forms of work to cope with unemployment, has caused the European Community to take an interest. A resolution on Voluntary Work passed by the European Parliament on 16th December 1983 stated that volunteering or voluntary work has at least the following four characteristics: 'It is not obligatory and it is socially relevant, it is unpaid, and it is carried out with some degree of organisation'. The resolution estimated that in most Member States 15% of the population are involved in voluntary work. It asked the Commission to carry out a survey of the extent of voluntary work, and to support innovative and possibly experimental projects that involved voluntary organisations, with priority for projects involving the elderly, the poor, and the unemployed. Work was also to be done to develop a set of rules defining the nature and condition of voluntary work, and to establish a European Forum on Voluntary Work.

The European Forum now exists in the shape of Volonteurope, which is 'a committee to encourage unpaid voluntary action in countries of the European Community'. The Committee brings together leading members of organisations that provide a platform for voluntary activity in each country. In an edition of its Journal (Number 5), the Committee investigates the issue of which work might be paid, and reaches a number of conclusions that provide a useful overview of the state of voluntary work.

2.2 Ease of participation

The first important point Volonteurope makes is that volunteering is a European-wide activity, though it varies in the degree of support available. It is apparently most organised in the UK and least in the Scandinavian countries (where there has been a strong tendency to professionalise all work). Volonteurop argue that voluntary action is not generally doing the same job as paid work and is not therefore in competition. Voluntary work is characterised by the ease with which those who want can participate (with no formal qualifications needed). The possibilities of part-time involvement, and the lack of formal labour contracts make it accessible to people who might otherwise be prevented from taking on a job (by responsibilities for children, for instance, or antisocial tendencies). It can also employ people who lack experience or qualifications, like many of the young unemployed. For example most of the workers in the Ecological Cycle Foundation project in Arnhem which collects waste food in horse-drawn carts would never ordinarily secure a job (see **Appendix B**). They are motivated by factors such as friendship, and the desire to do something interesting, and this can be an advantage in some situations. This also means, however, that volunteering can suffer from the disadvantage of lack of reliability or continuity, and almost inevitably carries an 'amateurish' image.

Voluntary work thus could have an important role to play in providing unemployed people with work experience. This is because of the lack of any threshold qualifications which enables virtually anyone to 'lend a hand' (providing there is some one to organise them). However, in practice this tends to be the exception rather than the rule. A British survey found that the rate of participation of employed people in voluntary work (18%) was almost twice that of unemployed people, and the situation is similar in other countries. This point is developed further in Chapter 4.

2.3 Community service

The part-time and somewhat unpredictable nature of volunteering led Volonteurope to conclude that it is best suited to work that involves human contact, such as help in the home and caring jobs, rather than work where the individual is indispensable and has to be available at a particular time. Recreation, education, and social rehabilitation are also considered well-suited to being undertaken by volunteers. However, its precise role varies from country to country. Thus in England the lower level of magistrates are unpaid, and it is regarded as an honour or social duty to be a Justice of the Peace. In Holland (and many other countries) play groups are largely run by volunteers (10,000 paid people and 40,000 volunteers). In Belgium homework projects are run by volunteers for pupils who are expelled from school. In general, work that requires a long education and is technically complicated, such as being a doctor, is paid. In contrast, work that is voluntary tends to require time rather than qualifications, and often includes tasks such as visiting people who are isolated, or raising money and serving on boards. There is almost invariably a sense that the work is in some way of service to others, or helps to create a better community. It can often involve working alongside paid staff. There are also cases of professionals acting as volunteers or working for reduced rates.

While this distinction may be too simplistic for general use, it is clear from this analysis that a major function of voluntary work is providing people with the satisfaction of doing something useful with their spare time. As such it is closely connected to leisure and educational activities which could also be seen as work, for example organising a tennis tournament, or studying to become an expert in something unusual. However, voluntary work also performs several other functions that are of potentially greater economic importance. Thus, voluntary action is often the main means of pioneering new services or forms of organisation. It is not government which generally leads, by passing laws or allocating funds, but voluntary organisations, who set up initiatives to tackle new problems, which then get publicised and taken up. Voluntary action therefore includes within its scope radicals who are seeking to change the world, as well as reformists and straightforward old-fashioned philanthropists.

The voluntary sector is sometimes treated by policy-makers as a cohesive group of organisations, rather like the public and private sectors, joined together by the motive of serving others. In fact it embraces a wide range of types of organisation with different management issues and with access to different types of help. Far from being a single homogeneous sector, three main types of initiative have been identified, which can be called local initiatives, intermediaries, and national voluntary organisations.

2.4 Local initiatives

Local environmental initiatives by community groups tend to be associations of people who have a common interest, and who apply the principles of mutual aid and self-help to improve their surroundings. They come into existence when people band together to draw attention to a need. For example, the Friends of the Marolles in Brussels was set up in 1959 to fight against slums. A group such as this may then want to do more than volunteers can do in their spare time. They may well become aware of the availability of grants from government or foundations that enable them to employ one or more workers. This stage usually represents a major transition, like going from a chrysalis to a butterfly, the Marolles Development Company later went on to launch projects for recycling television sets and cleaning offices (though it was later hampered by the loss of its subsidy).

Each local environmental initiative will have a particular constituency that is serves, and these can fall into a number of different categories:

a) **neighbourhood associations**, which include resident and tenant associations and amenity societies, are concerned with the well-being of people in a particular locality such as a street or a housing estate. Their main concern is usually with threats to the environment, such as a new road scheme, proposals for demolishing a group of buildings, or with the poor standards of maintenance

b) **ethnic groups**, bring together members of a particular racial minority in an area. They are usually concerned with a very wide range of needs as well as the special problems of discrimination and difficulties with adjusting to the national way of life, language and rules

c) **social action centres** have a local constituency, but seek to meet a multitude of needs. They are therefore more professionally based than the other community groups. Indeed, they often serve as 'intermediaries', providing expertise for groups within an area

d) **special interest groups** include for example, wildlife groups, urban studies centres, energy centres and groups involved with historic buildings and industrial archaeology.

The categories often overlap. What they have in common is their local focus i.e. part or all of a district, and their responsibility to a membership of essentially 'ordinary' people.

They are often dependent on public funding for any staff positions, which are usually short term and unpredictable. They generally work in isolation from each other, though in some cases there are federations which aim to bring groups together. The isolated and inevitably small scale nature of most groups, and their lack of coverage in the national media makes it hard to know what they are doing or achieving, compared with, say, national pressure groups. Yet as the case studies demonstrate, they can have a major impact on the way areas develop, mobilising many times their own resources.

2.5 National voluntary organisations

The term voluntary association can be used to cover all forms of voluntary work. However, there is a clear difference between the local initiative that is 'grassroots' based, and the branch of a national voluntary organisation concerned with serving a specific set of needs, such as the World Wildlife Fund. In the case of national voluntary organisations, the role of volunteers is often confined to acting as assistants to paid staff or raising funds. Of course, all organisations have to start somewhere, and many established national organisations started off as local initiatives. But others are almost like an arm of government, and this tendency is being reinforced in situations where governments back national organisations in running public employment schemes. The advantage to government is that such bodies are seen as reliable and, for example, will not abuse public funds. But it is probably these bodies that are most likely to represent a threat to the use of paid staff. For example, a strike in a hospital over the cut-backs in services may cause a voluntary organisation to take on the responsibilities of looking after the sick. A cut-back in the maintenance of parks or open spaces as has happened in Belgium, for example, could lead to something similar.

As far as environmental groups are concerned there is also a great deal of difference between well established bodies like the National Trust and Friends of the Earth, which both have equivalents in most European countries, and organisations who are committed to more narrow interests and who tend to have a great struggle to survive. It is the latter which form the main focus of this report, in view of their greater involvement in development work as opposed to campaigning.

2.6 Intermediaries and resource centres

A third type of organisation are those bodies involved with providing technical assistance and representation to community groups and voluntary organisations at local, regional and national levels. There is a rapidly growing number of these 'intermediaries', whose function is to provide help and encouragement, particularly to projects that are starting up. This is often referred to as 'enabling' and the bodies themselves are sometimes called 'resource centres'. For example, in the UK, where the support system is most developed, there is not only a National Council for Voluntary Organisations, concerned with representing the voluntary sector in government and with providing a central source of expertise, but also local Councils for Voluntary Service covering the same areas as local authorities in all the main parts of the country. In France, in contrast, the national organisations were only founded in the 1980s, and there is little organisation at the city level, where voluntary action often encounters resistance.

The kinds of services provided by resource centres include help with accounting, with fund-raising, and in some cases with obtaining land and buildings. Local Councils of Voluntary Service in Britain also provide information on sources of public finance and some run training sessions for the staff of voluntary organisations. There are also specialist 'resource centres' dealing purely with environmental concerns. They include national bodies like the Civic Trust in the UK and Italia Nostra in Italy. In the UK there are now over 70 'community technical aid centres' providing architectural and other related skills to local initiatives. Some examples in other countries were also uncovered in the research, like Planerladen, providing planning aid to residents in North Dortmund, and Inter-Environment in Brussels, which is one of four federations serving groups of associations in the major cities. There are also more specialist bodies serving particular networks of interests, like the National Federation of City Farms and Community Gardens in the UK, which is now developing links throughout Europe. Equally there are some 'not for profit' firms of consultants whose activities fall under this category. Intermediaries or resource centres are one way of overcoming the lack of technical expertise on the part of individual projects, and of raising performance standards in the voluntary sector generally. They also provide a convenient way in which government can channel resources into voluntary action without taking any risks. There is, however, another perspective, and that is the danger that too much effort can go into support staff and not enough into direct action.

2.7 Development trusts and community businesses

The final category of organisation comprises voluntary organisations that sell a product or service. There are a growing number of groups that seek to act entrepreneurially but in the public interest, by promoting socially beneficial forms of development. These can cover the full range of environmental concerns from preserving old buildings to providing services that meet specific social needs such as insulating the homes of the elderly or collecting waste paper. Such bodies combine an income from selling services with grants from the provision of public services. They can arise from local concerns, as for example with Pennine Heritage which forms one of the British case studies (see **Appendix B**) which was started by two university lecturers. Alternatively they can be promoted by government departments concerned with the environment or countryside. A good example is the expanding network of Groundwork Trusts that are promoting environmental improvement schemes in different parts of England and Wales, and which were originally set up by the Countryside Commission in partnership with local authorities and local voluntary and business interests.

Community businesses are not necessarily distinct from the other categories. Thus a project may well start as an unincorporated community group, and then go on to set up a trust or a limited company to pursue a specific project. The importance of forming such a body relates to insuring the members of the association against claims for damage or liability if the project fails, and also taking on the responsibilities of being an employer. Increasinglys voluntary associations are interested in setting up ventures that generate revenue and help to support the parent body once initial grants run out.

2.8 Conclusions

Voluntary work is essentially work that is not obligatory, is largely unpaid, and involves some degree of organisation. The various national reports have shown that despite considerable differences in the institutions and environment, there is a common interest at a European level in the role voluntary groups can play in initiating and running projects that improve the environment. Voluntary organisations have more in common with each other than they do with either government or private businesses, and therefore can be seen as forming a distinct 'third force'. However there are still major differences within the sector between the different types of organisation involved. In particular, local initiatives run by community groups are very different from national voluntary organisations. It is local initiatives that concern us most in this study. This is because they involve the beneficiary in their work (and are therefore more fulfilling and less likely to be patronising). Another type of voluntary organisation is intermediaries or resource centres providing technical assistance. In some cases voluntary organisations go on to set up development trusts or community businesses that seek to act entrepreneurially but in the public interest.

3   IMPACT ON THE ENVIRONMENT

While this research project has uncovered some fascinating and important examples of how voluntary action can contribute to resolving environmental problems, many will question whether this is an area that justifies more resources (or even attention) in the light of so many competing demands. Yet it is also possible that the action of voluntary groups, on a necessarily small scale, offers insights into ways of tackling more fundamental problems that hold the centre of the policy arena. Indeed, the voluntary sector may well include the pioneers or pilots who both help to show the way, and also identify the obstacles to progress. So while there is no way in which the voluntary sector can be seen as a substitute for publicly financed work, initiatives by local people merit serious consideration by policy makers. While the nature and urgency of environmental problems vary from area to area and from country to country, five general problems seem to affect most of the Northern European countries and these are:

o   the challenge of urban decay,
o   the problem of urban sprawl,
o   demands for a better quality of life,
o   the threat to our heritage,
o   and the need for jobs.

This chapter therefore considers, why environmental issues have sparked off so many voluntary groups.

3.1 The challenge of urban decay

The problems of urban decay, which once were thought only to affect the UK and the USA, are now of concern to most of the industrialised countries. The problems include a growing polarisation between rich and poor areas, as places that grew up around industry in the 19th century have lost their purpose, particularly those dependent on heavy industry and the docks. Thus a city like Hamburg faces the same problems in its dockland areas as do cities like London and Liverpool, while the British textile cities of Leeds and Bradford have gone through the same process of adjustment that seems to be affecting French cities like Lille and Roubaix. Urban decay has a strong environmental dimension. Factories and other commercial activities closing down leave vast areas of wasteland if they are not reused. Buildings left uncared for, after a while begin to rot or go up in flames. It is significant that this problem no longer just applies to Britain and the USA, though it varies in significance (and thus is not seen as much of a problem in Italy).

Faced with problems on a scale not seen since the last World War, cities find it hard to adjust to a new role. New and growing commercial organisations prefer greenfield sites, away from all the problems and extra costs associated with declining areas. Regeneration becomes increasingly difficult. The resources are no longer available locally to redevelop run-down areas, once the economic base of a city has declined beyond a certain point. Excessive levels of unemployment and a drab or derelict environment then make people feel helpless. They aggravate the processes that lead to social tension, violence and drug addiction. The vicious circle becomes inescapable.

The economic arguments for investing in regeneration are bound up with the social costs of doing nothing. For the costs are increasing all the time, while the resources are not. The enormous waste associated with this process by itself should provide the justification for acting. But too few people are involved for the political pressures to be sufficient to focus enough resources, except as palliatives when the areas occasionally erupt. The communities themselves are divided, the problems of ethnic minorities adding fuel to the fire. The spectre of parts of Belfast and Brooklyn could in time haunt many more of our European centres if the sores are left untreated. One value of local voluntary groups is that they involve people in caring for their environment and can sometimes achieve results that neither local governments nor private business are able to. A good example in the UK is Free Form Arts Trust, a local intermediary group specialising in community arts, who involve residents of old housing estates in for example creating beautiful mosaics. The pay-off should be seen in the reduced rate of vandalism and social malaise.

3.2 The problem of urban sprawl

At the same time as investment drains out of the cities, particularly the industrial and working class residential districts, the areas of land covered by buildings continue to increase. There are threats to traditional mixed neighbourhoods on the edge of central business districts. The expanding demands for offices in some cities, that can afford to pay more for the sites, leads to the loss not only of historic buildings but also employment and whole ways of life. At the edge of our cities, the very countryside that should provide recreational facilities or produce food, becomes blighted until permission is secured for building on it. The small towns and villages in particular in many European countries are losing their traditional character as pressures for development cause land to be nibbled away at the edge. The pressures are greatest in the 'sunbelt' of the South. In retrospect we may seem little more advanced than nomadic tribes, who continually move their habitation when they have exhausted the land, or the people of the 'Dark Ages', when the Roman Empire crumbled and both culture and security disappeared for a while.

The concern to protect nature from attack forms a major motive for many of the voluntary groups covered in the case studies. For example, there is a League of Young

Germans for the Protection of Forests which organises work camps. Such groups may also mobilise people to oppose new roads and housing developments that destroy natural habitats or they may be involved in practical initiatives. There is particular concern in most parts of Europe over the loss of amphibians and insects as a result of the spread of roads, the loss of hedgerows, and the use of pesticides. There is also the acute problem of the loss of both trees and damage to the facades of historic buildings as a result of 'acid rain'. Such interests are often very specialised. For example, the French Fund for the Protection of Predatory Birds (FIR) has some 500 voluntary workers. A wide range of local and national organisations are involved with wildlife. For example in Britain, associations include County Wildlife Trusts, the British Trust for Conservation Volunteers, the Royal Society for the Protection of Birds, as well as projects with a very specialised focus, either in terms of a particular aspect of nature or a particular piece of land. Thus, the London Wildlife Trust, as an example, has a membership of 4,500 and a staff of over 30.

3.3 Demands for a better quality of life

Downward trends in our cities take place against a great concern to improve the quality of life, and that puts special emphasis on the environment. More than a century ago most people could take their environment for granted. Buildings were expected to last many life times. Traditional methods of agriculture kept the landscape looking familiar. Today what is familiar and valued disappears before our eyes. The very monuments of the whole Italian artistic heritage have to be protected with chemical film against erosion from the exhaust fumes of cars, while the level of noise vibration does further damage. The countryside too is under threat as fields are built on and hedgerows pulled down to cut costs and increase profits.

It is reasonable to assume, following the idea of a hierarchy of needs, that once the basic needs for food, shelter and clothing are satisfied, other higher needs begin to surface.

These can include the conservation of familiar buildings and the countryside, the maintenance of clean air and water, and so on. Just as in the 19th century the pressures of epidemics led to the great public works schemes for piped drinking water and sewers, so today's pressures are calling for similar action on a grand scale to provide a more humane environment and better recreational facilities, as well as creating new habitats for wildlife. Some of the wildlife groups in particular see themselves engaged in the equivalent of a crusade to defend nature against attack and to combat pollution. However, the objectives of protecting nature and promoting economic growth do not have to conflict. It is in the economic interest of the older industrial towns to present a greener and cared for image to the outside world if they are to attract or retain private investment. Improving the environment should therefore be treated as a mainstream activity and not just a temporary fad.

3.4 The threat to the heritage

Along with the decline in economic activity goes the loss of the resources to occupy and maintain buildings. Capital accumulated in the past, which is effectively a free gift to this generation, could be thrown away if nothing is done to halt the process of decline. Three particular problems deserve to be singled out which could also generate considerable amounts of socially useful work. The first problem is the lack of maintenance of large housing estates, which particularly imperils housing in public ownership. Many estates form a kind of open prison, whose residents lack any alternatives or control over their lives. Yet there is evidence that often, with the right management and some investment, such buildings can be turned into homes which people want to live in. There is a vast amount of work to be done in improving the environment in which the more disadvantaged people live. The process can enable local people to exercise more control over their lives, and thus achieve self-respect and a sense of fulfilment. This particularly applies to the neglected common spaces between buildings. For example in Dortmund in Germany, groups of women tenants have been organising to 'green' courtyards formerly covered with tarmac. Similarly, in an isolated extensive housing estate in Oldham in England, children have been formed into the Sholver Rangers to improve the environment around the buildings.

The second problem, which now applies in most of the EC member states, is the problem of empty and under-utilised industrial buildings. Many are of no real economic value (even though they may carry a high financial value in the books of the company concerned). But some at least form part of a heritage that should be in trust for future generations. There are now sufficient examples of 'adaptive reuse' - imaginative schemes for turning old mills and warehouses, for example, into workspace for small firms, unusual homes, and places of recreation - to show that it is not necessary to abandon the buildings to the elements. Yet there is a real danger of buildings of great beauty and historic interest being sacrificed to short-term interests. Encouragingly in both France and the UK, and to a lesser extent in other countries, the idea of 'industrial tourism' is being used to change attitudes and generate new forms of work. There are also techniques like the inventory of vacant industrial premises prepared by Inter-Environment in Brussels, which can help tackle the problem under the slogan of 'do not throw away, instead reuse the industrial heritage'.

A third problem, which falls outside the scope of voluntary action, involves the infra-structure of sewers, rivers, roads and pavements, many of which are in urgent need of repair or replacement. Often they interact with other goals such as improving the quality of water or the look of urban areas (by for example undergrounding telephone wires). Not only is the Victorian system of sewers collapsing in many British towns, but the condition of the beaches falls below the minimum European standards. The situation in the Mediterranean is no better, and it appears that the sea is dying in parts of the North Sea and the Baltic. While control over pollution often involves massive capital investment, there are opportunities for developing small scale recreational facilities that will help to generate new activity to justify the investment, such as, for example, wind-surfing centres or fishing on water reservoirs.

3.5 Need for jobs

All of the above factors could be shrugged off as concerns of special interests or minorities who sometimes have only themselves to blame. But one over-riding factor about which all can agree is the need to generate worthwhile or satisfying employment on a major scale if people's self-respect is not to break down. The OECD has drawn attention to 'the end of full-time employment and the need for a new outlook on professional life'. Action to improve the environment could therefore be justified now because of the scope for rapidly generating employment for precisely the people who are most likely to be unemployed. It may also be essential for stopping vandalism and neglect and promoting confidence and investment. Environmental work is typically labour intensive. Renovating buildings requires far more labour in relation to capital than building afresh. So too does making productive use of small areas of wasteland (for example where a couple of houses once stood). Much of the manual work is relatively unskilled and can be used to gain not only useful practical skills but also experience of working in a group. There is also the satisfaction of having achieved something when a derelict building is renovated and turned to community use. There are now plenty of examples to show that with adequate supervision and leadership unemployed people can undertake impressive schemes. For example, in the UK development trusts like Pennine Heritage and the Ironbridge Gorge Museums Trust have converted historic industrial buildings into workshops using labour on temporary 'job creation' schemes. It seems that voluntary groups and local initiatives are more likely to use people on 'job creation' schemes than large employers, like local authorities, in part because they have little choice, but also because they are more flexible.

Similar arguments apply to measures involving resource conservation. Collecting waste paper or recycling materials like glass is essentially labour intensive, and so too is insulating the roofs of houses to stop heat loss. It is also something that produces a social as well as a commercial value, neither of which by themselves would generally be sufficient to lead people to action unless they are combined. For example, in the Netherlands, a

500 year old watermill in Arnhem has been restored to grind grain again and to act as a visitor centre, and some 24 volunteers are now working, typically for periods of 8-10 hours a week (though it has proved difficult to maintain the initial level of interest). Hence there is a need for initiatives with multiple objectives (environmental, economic and social). In searching for ways of improving the future of cities and stopping them sprawl, environmental work can provide not only a mechanism that meets a whole series of priority objectives simultaneously, but also generates employment and training opportunities in the process. It is therefore clear that the environment is not just a matter for a few cranks, or for when times are better.

3.6 Conclusions

Voluntary work can make a significant impact on some of the current European concerns. It can help to tackle the problems of urban decay by enabling local people to influence their environment. It can reduce the problem of urban sprawl by conserving and creating natural habitats. It can improve the quality of life by providing a more humane and cared for environment. It can alleviate the threat to our heritage by making housing estates liveable, by reusing historic industrial buildings, and by securing better value from investment in the infrastructure. Finally it can help create new jobs in resource conservation and in projects that have multiple objectives.

4   THE ROLES VOLUNTARY GROUPS PLAY

The case studies established not only a very wide range of types of work, but also the many different roles which voluntary groups can play in relation to the above problems - often at the same time. It would be wrong to think that all local initiatives want to, or are able to grow (any more than the small and medium sized enterprise, which they sometimes resemble). However, a certain pattern emerged from some of the case studies in terms of the way groups can evolve. The word 'group', incidentally, has been used as a general term, though organisations can vary from a loose association to a registered company with branches all over a country.

4.1 Protesters and campaigners

Whereas those involved in recreational and various forms of cultural association often come together to enjoy each others company, the impetus for the formation of many voluntary environmental groups tends to be opposition to some external threat. This can range from concern over nuclear power at one level, essentially national issues, to the possible loss of a natural habitat, an old building or a neighbourhood area of a city, which are in contrast local issues. Similarly, tactics can range from conventional lobbying to mass demonstrations and dramatic events that draw attention to the group's aims, such as a neighbourhood festival.

It is easy to dismiss much of this activity as negative or reactionary. Often such groups seem to be delaying progress for what is a minority interest. Yet, it should be remembered, such groups of activists may express much more widely held beliefs and be in the vanguard of change. Also in the environmental field, advocates of 'green' policies have managed to achieve political power in Germany, and are beginning to exercise considerable influence in a number of other countries. The work done in researching the issues, presenting alternatives, organising meetings, and generating a climate of opinion can be an indispensable part of the democratic process. It is often the case after environmental disasters, such as the destruction of traditional neighbourhoods and their replacement by high rise blocks of flats, that people wish they had listened to those presenting the alternative case. While groups who only played a campaigning role were seen as outside the concern of this research project, it appeared that all groups are involved in campaigning to some extent. But after a time groups have to move beyond protest to doing something practical if they are to retain support from their membership and from sponsors.

4.2 Missionaries

A natural extension of the protest and pressure group role is to produce and disseminate information that explains the cause and wins adherents. This can range from simple cyclostyled leaflets to sophisticated magazines, like Italy's Aeron, with a circulation of over 300,000 and an estimated one and a half million readers. Many of the publications are distributed to members, and do not reach a wider audience, but the scale can still be considerable. For example, Britain's National Trust has a million members, while the Civic Trust has affiliated groups in almost every town who receive their magazine Heritage Outlook. Others depend on securing sponsorship from research foundations or the public affairs departments of large companies in order to publicise the results of research into new initiatives; thus Shell UK has funded the publication of a very attractive booklet on raising funds for environmental projects as part of its 'Better Britain' campaign.

The reliance entirely on volunteers usually begins to break down as activities grow. In such cases, what starts as a voluntary group begins to become an employer, as it takes on specialist workers to extend its functions. Such roles are normally dependent on grants, which are typically for limited periods, which in turn creates fresh problems for the organisation as it seeks to expand its role in order to maintain public interest and financial support. In such cases, some income will come from the sale of goods and services. For example, the British National Trust has shops in all its main attractions, while a City Farm may sell cheese and vegetables grown on the land it occupies. A few projects have sought to become totally self-sufficient, like the Energy and Environment Centre in Eldagsen, Germany, which supports 15 people. But in general the proportion of revenue from users or beneficiaries is small in relation to overall operating costs, and almost never covers the development budget. There is in many cases scope for increasing the level of commercial income, if the group later seeks to set up community businesses, and introduce good management practices into its work. However, it is still practically impossible for such projects to cover more than a fraction of their costs in this way.

4.3 Promoters and animateurs

Many groups seek to undertake physical projects which directly improve the environment. The motives vary, but they can include providing a facility which people will use and enjoy, thus both meeting a local need and also helping to maintain community spirit. A prominent example is the series of temporary gardens that were developed in Covent Garden in the heart of London, during the period of the area's redevelopment. These were developed by the Covent Garden Community Association, a voluntary organisation engaged in fighting plans that involved the loss of traditional businesses or that did not benefit the residential community. The gardens, which were undertaken by volunteers, helped to make the association a force to be reckoned with. They provided a basis for events, such as festivals, which attracted supporters and drew publicity. They also (though this was not their purpose) helped to produce a creative 'alternative' environment which attracted 'pioneering' businesses, like film makers and designers, into the area. Later the existence of green spaces instead of wasteland probably encouraged new commercial development, thus ironically eliminating most of the gardens in the process.

But there is a further role and benefit of such ventures, and that is a demonstration of the principles underlying the group. There is an English phrase 'actions speak louder than words'. Practical projects, on the ground, can be used to symbolise not only what a group is fighting for, but also to create a sense of achievement or shared purpose which binds the group together. A lone windmill or triple glazing in a house may not mean much in terms of energy saved, but it can act as an example of what a conservation group is fighting for. Similarly the involvement of young children in planting trees can develop their interest in nature, and secure the support of their parents. Good examples are the Belgian Friends of the Forest de Soignes, and Concours-Qualité Quartiers in Liege which is a competition run by a local authority to provide materials for schemes devised by groups of residents.

As the German report stated, describing what are called citizen's initiatives, 'unlike the local urban projects of the early 1970s the main feature is no longer missionary zeal, but the subjective dimension of being effective as a local resident, of having ones own ideas, and of the necessity to initiate and implement actions and projects by relying on one's own resources.' It also seems to be true that a track record gained in one project, however small, overcomes scepticism in public authorities and helps to attract resources for doing something bigger. Thus it is common for groups to see their initial efforts on land available on a temporary basis swept away by development, but then to obtain larger areas of land, and on a more long-term basis. Often the groups act as 'animateurs' bringing dead areas to life, just as a promoter might use an empty stage for performances. This finding has important implications for how voluntary groups can become more successful.

4.4 Environmental managers

As the scale of achievement grows, so too does the amount of work involved in maintaining what has been developed and serving the public. For example, visitors to industrial museums, steam railways or even some nature reserves, want to see a well cared for site, and to be offered refreshments and things to buy. This in turn creates work, albeit unpaid, for more volunteers. There are hundreds of examples in the UK, and the idea seems to be spreading through Europe. For example, the Compagnie du Canal du Centre was set up in 1977 in Belgium following trips to the UK. It now runs five trip boats and employs some 30 or so permanent staff, many of whom were formerly volunteers or unemployed. While patterns vary from country to country, the main role of voluntary work seems to be in the activities that can be done when time is available, rather than being fitted into a regular time slot. These include helping to raise funds, running the 'supporters' club', and acting as attendants in dealing with the public. Such functions do not substitute for regular staff, but rather extend what is possible. Thus in European state museums it is normal to see paid staff simply acting as guards to prevent treasures being stolen or damaged. But in independent museums (and in public museums in the USA), volunteers work with the public in interpreting the past. Thus volunteers could be seen at one time reenacting the roles of the original workers in the Ironbridge Gorge Museum, England, or acting as guides in the industrial museum of Le Creusot, France. For many of the volunteers this enables them to develop a hobby and do something practical for a cause in which they believe.

As the activities of such projects grow, and the numbers of customers or users rises, so too does the opportunity to create 'community businesses.' Community businesses seek to meet a local need and also to produce social benefits which are often 'bought' by local authorities. Such ventures can enable people, who start as volunteers or workers on a publicly supported employment scheme, to go into business on their own account or as a cooperative with others. For example, the cafe at Windmill Hill City Farm in England is run as a profit centre, and is expected to become independent in time (see

Appendix B). There are now small businesses restoring old pieces of machinery, or providing facilities for tourists, which have all started on the back of environmental groups' efforts. Undoubtedly such schemes provide a good and safe grounding in what is involved in running a business, and enable the 'plunge' into self-employment to be taken in easy stages.

Some projects, such as wildlife trusts, essentially see their role as looking after a particular landscape of wildlife value and, in some cases, wildlife or woodland trusts may acquire land or else occupy it on a licence which allows temporary access, and makes them responsible for insurance. However, there is some evidence that urban voluntary groups are better at promoting schemes than maintaining them, and, indeed, it is often the challenge of overcoming bureaucracy that keeps people together. However, if the community is not involved at the beginning, it is less likely to take an interest in caring for what is provided. It may well be generally true, as the French report suggests, that 'there is a division between the work of thinking up the initiatives, which is the task of the volunteer leaders in the association, who also have paid jobs, and the other work, which is increasingly done by young unemployed people'.

4.5 Developers

As projects grow, some groups begin to run schemes that involve not only volunteers but also temporary workers. These tend to be development projects in which land and buildings are improved and new facilities are created. In such a case they should not be a threat to regular employees. They can over time enable a voluntary group to build up a substantial capital in terms of land, buildings and facilities under local control. Probably the largest example covered in the case studies looked at is Ironbridge Gorge Museums Trust in the UK, which supports several hundred temporary workers at any one time as well as some 100 paid staff. However, in the process it is worth noting that the voluntary ethos and contribution can easily become lost, leading to conflict. A similar experience has occurred in France in the Ecomusée de Haute Alsace.

Such projects can make a major environmental and economic impact, particularly when they are combined with properly trained staff, professional management, and an adequate budget for materials. For example, in the UK, major parts of the canal system, which had been abandoned, are now being reopened to provide a tourism and recreational facility. Similarly, but on a smaller scale, in Bailleul, France, a former municipal rubbish tip has been converted into a natural wooded area by young people. One trust in the UK, Pennine Heritage, has not only refurbished old buildings, but also publishes a magazine which aims to give a sense of pride to what had become a very run-down area (see **Appendix B**). It can, of course, be argued that such ventures would never be viable without extensive public subsidies, that they indulge minority enthusiasms, and that they do little to contribute to more basic human needs. Furthermore, perhaps because of the availability of land, many are concentrated outside the towns and cities with the worst problems. Indeed, it is often harder to launch the same project in urban areas because trades unions are more concerned about the use of temporary employment schemes. Nevertheless, such projects have demonstrated the scope for reclaiming derelict land and abandoned buildings, and putting them to uses in which the community secures some benefits (if only that it no longer has to live with a dangerous eyesore). They also help to bring communities together, which is not only valuable in its own right but reduces vandalism. A good example of what can be done by voluntary effort alone is the project in a suburb of Lyon to construct garages and a repair workshop, which involved 12 different nationalities and a high proportion of young people.

Sometimes a final stage is reached when a project proves so successful that it is taken over either by the State or by private business. This has for example happened in the case of the restoration of the Rochdale Canal. The 550 member strong Rochdale Canal Society now concentrates on the role of acting as a 'champion', leaving it to the local authorities to organise the restoration work, which employed 350 temporary workers at one time.

4.6 Conclusions

Voluntary work has an important contribution to play in meeting current European concerns. It can help to tackle the challenge of urban decay, the problem of urban sprawl, the demands for a better quality of life, the threat to our European heritage, and the need for more employment creation. Such activity is important at the European level because the problems of economic adjustment affect almost all the European countries and certainly all the industrial towns and cities. There is also scope for disseminating good practice and launching new initiatives that mobilise resources on a major scale. Support for voluntary action could give an EC environmental programme a new dimension and one that would not duplicate existing efforts. The role voluntary groups play can vary along a continuum. Often groups start as protest and pressure groups, then go on to play a missionary role, and provide recreational facilities to broaden their support. Maintenance is also a function but one that voluntary groups are not particularly keen to take on except as an adjunct to their development work. The final stage is to promote development schemes that transform the environment and attract new activities or uses.

5   VOLUNTARY WORK AND EMPLOYMENT

This chapter examines the contribution voluntary work in the environment can make to employment. It deals in turn with:

   o job satisfaction,
   o job creation,
   o preparation for employment,
   o new work,
   o and job replacement.

5.1 Job satisfaction

Statistics on volunteering are limited, and so use has been made of the surveys most readily available. Several surveys have shown that voluntary work is more prevalent among the employed than the unemployed and among the higher socio-economic classes. Hence, volunteering is not primarily a way of filling the time of the unemployed. Instead, it seems to be largely a way of allowing people with occupations to fill their spare time productively by doing something they enjoy in the company of people who share a similar interest. A survey in the UK in 1984 showed that 250,000 volunteers carried out 1.6 million days of work on improving the environment (equivalent to the time of roughly 6,000 full-time employees). Interestingly, however, a French survey by CREDOC showed that the proportion of people in voluntary associations involved with the environment fell from 4.1% in 1978 to 1.6% in 1984, whereas sports in contrast rose from 15.4% to 17.5%.

The British surveys indicate that 1 in 5 people are involved in volunteering, though traditional 'social work' activities far outnumber environmental work. Figures for participation in voluntary work in other countries include an estimate of 15% of the population in Belgium and 45% in the Netherlands (though definitions vary). There is an interesting contrast in one British survey between the characteristics of the traditional volunteer (that tend to reflect the conservative view of philanthropy), and the environmental volunteer, who is more concerned with changing society. A growing concern for the environment is leading to an escalating number of people involved in voluntary associations, though only a small proportion will be involved in practical action. Indeed most groups are run by a few activists, backed up by many more who simply read the newsletter or attend occasional meetings. Environmental voluntary work is only thought to involve 4% of the UK's population (and a similar proportion in Belgium). It seems likely that some people look to volunteering to provide an alternative to their normal work. For example, some people who work all week in an office welcome the chance of getting out in the country, and doing something that involves manual effort or what the Germans call 'dirty hands' work. Others want to use the same skills but in a task that is more meaningful or where they have more power. As mainstream work has become more and more cut off from the sense of making useful things or serving human needs, so voluntary work can provide a degree of compensation.

There is a case for considering voluntary work rather like we do sports, the arts or education, that is something worthwhile in its own right, and which forms part of the culture of a civilised society. Rather than being seen as 'do-gooding' (which necessarily limits its appeal), it can be seen as a way of obtaining enjoyment without acquiring and consuming goods or services. This has important implications for the design of mainstream jobs. The practice of 'seconding' managerial staff to work on voluntary projects, which has been adopted by many of the large companies in the UK, could become a means both of providing a more fulfilling career for executives and for sharing work round, rather than an exercise in corporate charity. However it is worth noting that most of the jobs involve 'brain rather than brawn', and that those who are least skilled are not typically benefitting from voluntary work.

5.2 Job creation

A major factor in the last few years throughout Europe has been the expansion of 'public works' programmes as a means of occupying the unemployed. This has led to the expansion of existing voluntary agencies who organise temporary 'job creation' projects, using money from the government to pay wages. Many of these projects are environmental, and thus avoid doing work that would produce private benefits or substitute for work that is already being done. A survey in 1984, found there were 46,000 places for unemployed people in the UK on environmental projects supported by the Manpower Services Commission, which amounted to over 23% of their Community Programme for the long-term unemployed, and the actual amount of work done was some four times the level produced by volunteers. In other countries, a similar picture emerges, with Germany and France probably being in the lead. However, a survey of publicly funded environmental improvement projects in Birmingham showed that relatively few were promoted by the voluntary sector, suggesting that local authorities are a far more significant force for change. There has been strong resistance from trades unions in some areas, but the most successful projects are the ones where community groups have secured acceptance for their role. The majority of the places were created by local authorities, often using national voluntary organisations such as the British Trust for Conservation Volunteers to manage the projects. (Since this report was prepared, the Manpower Services Commission has been turned into the Training Agency, and the Community Programme, replaced by Employment Training which has greatly reduced the role and effectiveness of voluntary organisations).

Environmental work lends itself to the creation of projects that use people on a temporary basis. It can also produce a sense of accomplishment when, for example, a derelict building is restored and turned into a community centre. The provision of employment for those who would otherwise remain unemployed can also provide a satisfaction. Equally important, it creates an outlet for the energies and talents of unemployed university graduates. Though many projects are individually small, the organisations involved can be quite large, and indeed many smaller projects find it impossible to comply with all the rules.

One reason for the rise of the large 'job creation' agencies are the problems of dealing with government funding, and of getting projects going. It is simply not economic for most small community groups to set projects up, and many of those who have been lured by the prospects of easy funding have lived to regret it. The problem of getting projects going and managing them is particularly acute in the case of environmental, as opposed to social or even economic, projects. This is because of the time taken securing agreement from landowners and planning authorities as case studies like Pennine Heritage in England demonstrate. An action research project undertaken by URBED (Urban and Economic Development Group) showed that some 50 meetings can be involved before a landscaping project can get underway, and this is too great a burden for the average voluntary organisation members' spare time.

While the growth of what might be called environmental development agencies offers some potential advantages in terms, for example, of their ability to employ qualified management and to organise training, the nature of some of the work undertaken needs to be questioned. Often projects may secure funding because they keep large numbers of people occupied (like clearing over-grown cemeteries, for example) rather than because they respond to community needs or provide good work experience. But in the absence of well qualified and motivated staff (or consultants) to act as project designers and enablers the chances are that the work carried out will be unimaginative and may soon deteriorate once the project finishes. Studies have shown that voluntary workers are far more interested in undertaking development projects than carrying out ongoing maintenance. Yet the low levels of skill available for planning projects can result in schemes that require high levels of continuing mainteinance (for example 'soft' landscaping).

The basic policy issue to be resolved, assuming that such work needs to be done, is whether an environmental project is best undertaken by the community groups, who identify the need, national voluntary organisations, who specialise in running temporary employment as training schemes, or local authorities, who can handle the ongoing maintenance, but who may lack the resources and sometimes the expertise.

5.3 Preparation for employment

One argument in favour of temporary employment schemes of the kind run by voluntary agencies is that they are a useful preparation for real jobs. Projects seem to vary greatly in the effort put into training and placing people in permanent jobs. The best have a good record, and often do a better job than statutory authorities because they are smaller and care more. However, there is a basic problem, which is that the bulk of the work involves simple manual tasks which do not provide the level of experience needed to secure employment. The pressure to do work in a labour intensive way means that there is little chance to learn how to use modern machines. Furthermore, unless the objectives and benefits are obvious, morale can soon lag, with the best people always leaving. The problems are compounded by the difficulties in providing adequate supervision, due to limits on funding, which causes groups to employ staff who are themselves often inadequate to supervise and motivate those without any skills or motivation.

It is not surprising, therefore, that many established voluntary organisations, who have seen well thought out plans set aside by all too frequent changes in government policy, have become wary of becoming employers. Concern was also felt in several of the case studies that volunteers were displaced by temporary workers, once the decision was taken to run a job creation scheme. This is a great pity because well planned and managed projects can undoubtedly achieve a great deal, as some of the case studies demonstrate.

5.4 New work

Now that it seems as if unemployment is a long-term phenomenon, a number of voluntary organisations have become interested in setting up what are called 'community businesses'. These seek to cover the costs of employing people from the sale of a product or service and have their basis in meeting local needs, and in involving members of the community on their boards. Often the customer will be the public sector, for example, through schools paying to take children to visit a city farm or independent museum. But the great difference is that they rely on the public sector supporting outputs rather than inputs through payment for services.

This interest is growing as voluntary groups seek to avoid over-dependence on grants. These include local organisations involved with recycling waste materials, insulating homes and renovating old machinery. They also include some national organisations such as the British Trust for Conservation Volunteers, who at one time employed some 350 members of staff, many of whom hold effectively permanent posts. However, such ventures can generally only work where they secure a wider market for what they are doing than the community in which they are based. Unfortunately, there is still a great deal of naivety and wishful thinking, where voluntary boards of management expect to be able to survive in a highly competitive world, using inexperienced workers and inadequate capital resources, to meet what are essentially social needs. The key to survival is securing grants for the social aspects of their work.

As well as the 'community business spin-offs', there are undoubtedly many other people who have been able to use the time on a publicly supported venture to develop their own ideas and make the contacts needed to set up a business. This also applies to members of the management committee. Thus voluntary projects can sometimes be an excellent training ground for running a small business, in sheltered but realistic conditions. Though not enough is known to establish whether this is a major source of new enterprise, an interesting pattern can be observed which could provide a model for work in a post-industrial society. After graduating from college, perhaps as ecologists, some idealistic young people may become involved as volunteers in a project that satisfies their interests. They contribute energy and whatever skills they already possess on a voluntary basis. In time an opening arises on a government funded job creation scheme. They then might go on to become paid workers, supervising others. Alternatively, they might become self-employed, selling their time to different projects or even joining a landscaping cooperative to provide a broader range of expertise, with the capacity to take on larger projects.

On similar lines, older people who have worked all their lives for large organisations may 'drop out' or be made redundant, and use the time to develop what had previously been a hobby into something that can generate an income. Often this will involve a 'portfolio' of jobs, with a bit of teaching, a bit of consultancy, a bit of manual work and so on. While it would be dangerous to exaggerate the scale on which this happens, undoubtedly some voluntary organisations are pioneering alternative life styles, and forms of work. For example, Windmill Hill City Farm in England, is located in a neighbourhood of Bristol, housing a number of alternative projects, including energy conservation and publishing.

Environmental projects can also stimulate or support new work through the impact they have on raising confidence and opening up new opportunities. The transformation of a derelict canal into a recreational waterway, for instance, creates some jobs for those involved in selling and maintaining boats, running hire cruisers and so on. It can also induce developers to create new facilities, like waterside inns or housing, and thus produces new economic activity in what had been considered a wasteland. Similarly a festival may not only change local attitudes to an area and develop community spirit, but may also attract the interest of businesses who are looking for workspace. The growth of tourism as an industry in older industrial areas is often only possible because of projects that have improved the environment and created new visitor attractions.

5.5 Job replacement

There is an understandable concern that the growth of the voluntary sector and temporary employment schemes will be used to substitute for properly paid permanent employment. As a result there has been strong resistance in some of the areas of highest unemployment to the use of temporary employment schemes. There has also been some resistance to the involvement of voluntary organisations in areas where local authorities have been faced with cut-backs on what they can do.

In the case studies, perhaps because the projects were innovative, the great bulk of the work was new, and different from what an established organisation would have undertaken. There are also checks to stop governments getting work done 'on the cheap'; thus each 'temporary work' project has to be approved by committees on which there are representatives of employers, unions and the voluntary sector. Also the main role of volunteers, once an employment scheme starts, tends to be on the management; for example in Pennine Heritage, a development trust in England, over 100 people participated in project working parties and management committees, while there were some 15 permanent paid staff.

A more serious problem is that resources may have been directed at creating temporary employment in some countries, at the expense of expanding other more needed activities that would have created employment in the process. Also maintenance jobs in local authorities have been hit by cut-backs in a number of European countries, for example park-keepers in some Belgian cities. A 'two nation' economy results, the one in which real wages rise fast, while in the other the problems of poverty intensify. As there are virtually no cases where voluntary groups can be successful in promoting schemes without some support from public authorities, particularly at the local level, it seems pointless to view them as alternatives. They should rather be seen as working in partnership with each other. However, care will be needed to stop 'job creation' schemes being used for maintenance, as opposed to development work, or for temporary jobs that offer no training or long-term employment prospects.

5.6 Conclusions

The main contribution of the voluntary sector to work is to create a more fulfilling life style for those who are already in work. But voluntary groups also play an important role in initiating and managing projects that provide temporary work for those who are unemployed. Some lead on to permanent jobs in new fields. Unfortunately, small voluntary groups often find that they are not suited to the role of acting as trainers, while volunteers can be displaced by the use of temporary workers. The main danger of substitution for permanent jobs is where local authorities are forced to cut back on activities like maintenance, and resources are used to support work of less value to the community.

6 STRENGTHS AND WEAKNESSES

This chapter is concerned with the situations in which voluntary action is most appropriate and with ways of improving the effectiveness of voluntary groups. It deals with the particular strengths and weaknesses of voluntary action that cut across national boundaries.

All the national reports were enthusiastic about the role voluntary groups can play in complementing statutory provision, despite the frequent weaknesses. Far from competing with or displacing either government or business, the general impression is that voluntary organisations meet needs that would not otherwise be met.

6.1 Community involvement

One of the main strengths of voluntary work is the scope for involving local people in both the planning and the provision of a service. There is a world of difference between a derelict site that is landscaped by an architect and a firm of contractors who live miles away with no local consultation, and the same site brought back to life by a community group who live on the spot and who commission or carry out the work as a client. Community involvement means working closely with the different groups who might use a site to establish their needs and viewpoints. It also means getting them involved in the process, which helps to build up skills and create a sense of achievement.

There is now evidence from studies that have been undertaken of community initiated and run projects, that such schemes take account of factors that would otherwise be ignored, and hence are less likely to be vandalised or neglected. In turn, those involved develop a sense of confidence, as well as practical skills, which lead them on to greater things, such as the unemployed member of the group getting a job, for example, or starting his or her own business. Thus one of the German case studies stressed the need to appraise projects not just by economic criteria, but by 'the confirmation of one's identity by doing something, or the setting of an example to one's descendants'. One of the great virtues of the voluntary sector is its sensitivity to those in greatest need, who might otherwise be cut off from the provision of services.

Such a process may happen readily in middle class neighbourhoods where owner-occupiers group together to protect the values of their property. But it is also clear that with the right animateur or community leader, the same process can occur in run-down working class areas. One of the UK case studies of the Provost Housing Estate showed that the employment of a 'community architect' ensured that an estate which was generally regarded as 'a problem' or 'sink' became a popular place to live, with a thriving community association. The Belgian case study of the Action Committee of the Marolles, a working class area in Brussels, also shows how the environment provides good raw material for the process of community development (**Appendix B**).

6.2 Multiple benefits

While many groups start with quite narrow goals, it is common for community groups to expand their horizons, and seek to promote projects that meet a range of needs. This is in contrast to both local authorities and private businesses who tend to pursue single or more narrow objectives. Thus, a project like Windmill Hill City Farm in England is in part concerned with improving the environment and stopping a piece of wasteland in a poor residential area from being used as a lorry park. But the project is also about community development and increasing the capabilities of local people to manage their own affairs. There is an economic dimension too, because of the jobs and training opportunities that are created, and spin-offs in terms of community businesses. While it would be wrong to exaggerate the impact such projects are having, the point is that voluntary environmental projects have the potential for acting as catalysts for local economic development and neighbourhood revival. It is the multiple nature of the objectives, incidentally, which often causes voluntary groups to resist the idea of measuring performance.

6.3 Pioneers and innovators

It is a well established fact in commercial enterprise that much innovation in industry tends to come from the smaller firms. In part this is because they identify gaps in the market that the larger organisations have missed or do not consider worth catering for. It is also because a business run by an individual entrepreneur tends to be more energetic and prepared to take risks, and is less concerned with keeping its colleagues happy. The same general principles are also likely to apply to social enterprises. Thus it tends to be the voluntary sector where new approaches are first tried out, and where successful these are taken up by the public sector. Such a process applied, for example, to the conversion of redundant industrial buildings into workspace for small firms in England, where some of the initial projects were backed by charitable foundations who tend to concentrate their limited resources on innovative ideas. Similarly, much of the innovation in the way museums are run, such as the concept of open air museums, or in approaches to education, such as the Italian Green Universities, has come from the voluntary sector.

One of the reasons why the voluntary sector is often responsible for innovation is that innovative individuals tend to avoid working for large organisations. Also, it is significant that innovation often comes from those who know very little about the subject and are therefore free from the constraints of 'conventional wisdom'. The need for rapid social innovation has never been greater, given the challenges of coping with a post-industrial society. Hence voluntary groups possess a strength which is highly relevant, and this particularly applies to those that emerge from the grassroots. For example, voluntary groups have pioneered radical ideas for transforming old areas, like urban forests, such as in Milan, or city farms, such as in Bristol (**Appendix B**). They have also sought to innovate in the way they manage themselves, trying out more participative approaches to management than would be the case in the public or private sectors.

6.4 Low overheads

Another factor working in favour of voluntary groups is their ability to survive on very limited budgets. Enthusiasm and the principle of 'making do' have to compensate for lack of resources. Thus voluntary groups work out of members' homes or in 'short-life' property that is awaiting demolition, often made available on favourable terms by sympathetic public bodies. Instead of a paid board of directors, they rely on a voluntary management committee. Such staff as there are generally receive lower salaries and fringe benefits than in the public or private sectors, while much of the work is undertaken by volunteers or people on job creation schemes. As the Belgian report points out, this willingness to work for lower pay and in more precarious conditions of employment represents a donation from the individual to the 'cause'. However, such practices tend to restrict involvement in the voluntary sector to those who are better off or who are prepared to live on very little.

The low level of overheads also forces organisations to be very flexible in what they do, changing the services provided to suit changing needs (or just as likely government priorities and regulations). This is in marked contrast to established local authorities, who are bound by the rules governing professions and the democratic process, both of which tend to slow things down. It is therefore often the case that voluntary organisations can provide services more cheaply than the statutory equivalent, particularly where an important variable is care and dedication.

6.5 Employment for the disadvantaged

Thirdly, though most environmental projects do not start with the objective of creating employment, this is often a useful side-effect of their being successful in their main objectives. Because voluntary groups are very limited in who they can attract as employees, the natural tendency is for them to end up employing those who would otherwise have difficulties securing employment. Thus, in France typical employees include conscientious objectors and prisoners on community service, as well as those funded under state 'job creation' and training schemes. Unemployed graduates in disciplines like ecology and planning are a major source of skilled staff. It is significant that in the larger and more established projects, the time put in by paid staff far exceeds the contribution of volunteers, who end up being involved largely in management and fund-raising.

Because environmental projects are relatively labour intensive and provide public benefits, they are natural candidates for state supported job creation schemes in most European countries. Though in the UK voluntary groups still account for a very small proportion of environmental improvement projects, environmental projects accounted for a high proportion of the projects undertaken under the Manpower Services Commission's Community Programme. Many of these projects were undertaken by national voluntary organisations who act rather like building contractors, and who have grown large as a result of responding to the government's special programmes. However, the situation varies greatly from country to country and for example in Italy it is only recently that the Ministry of Labour proposed 5,000 jobs relating to the environment.

There is an important conflict here between the needs of community groups, who are limited in what they can or want to do, and the needs of government departments who look for organisations that can 'deliver' national programmes without much civil service involvement. As a consequence, instead of resources going to support community groups, the tendency is for them to go to national voluntary organisations, who then provide local authorities with a subsidised workforce. Examples in the UK are the National Association for the Care and Resettlement of Offenders (NACRO) and Community Task Force, both of whom at any one time had over 5,000 'employees' on job creation schemes (though the number has reduced since the replacement of the Community Programme by Employment Training). In turn national programmes tend to lead to support for projects which are easy to administer and require little in the way of materials or equipment, such as clearing out old cemeteries, rather than projects which respond to community needs.

6.6 Commitment

One of the most distinctive factors about voluntary organisations, particularly new ones, is the commitment and energy of the originators The concept of the 'charismatic leader' or 'social entrepreneur' who acts as chairman and who provides the driving force needed to get a project going is becoming widely known; less obvious is the role played by other individuals who provide support and complementary skills, and who undertake the more prosaic jobs of serving as honorary secretary and treasurer. Many environmental projects are started by quite extraordinary people who believe strongly in a set of values which they want to prove in practice. Hence, they provide the necessary 'sweat equity,' to use an American expression, without counting the time and cost. Their vision in conceiving the project, and guts in committing themselves when all is uncertain, represent vital ingredients in launching major projects successfully. When environmental projects are completed they provide a sense of fulfilment for both individuals and groups.

6.7 Freedom of expression

A final strength or virtue of voluntary action is that it preserves the diversity of opinion that is essential to the maintenance of a free society. The group campaigning against the destruction of a wildlife habitat or historic building may be a costly nuisance to those who own the site, but can also be an essential mainstay of democracy. In a large number of areas, society has belatedly come to thank those who campaigned on behalf of basic environmental values, and who sought to demonstrate their commitment by organising demonstration projects, however small they might have been in relation to the size of the problem.

6.8 Vulnerability

Despite the potential strengths of voluntary groups, they in fact encounter considerable resistance from established organisations, particularly when they start up. This problem applies to all the countries studied, and so is as much a response to the nature of voluntary action as it is to the practices in any particular country. The criticisms made of voluntary groups seems to fall into four main areas.

The small scale nature of most voluntary groups, and their dependence upon a charismatic leader, makes them liable to collapse, particularly if they fail to make progress over a period of years. There are further problems for groups operating in working class or ethnic minority neighbourhoods, where the failure to obtain a grant can cause a project to lose its supporters because members lack the financial resources to keep going. Such community groups also suffer from lack of connections with those in power.

Projects are also susceptible to collapse when they expand rapidly, and employ people with differing values. Conflicts then arise between members of staff and management committees, which the group is unable to resolve, particularly when it adopts a demo-cratic management style. The high turnover of members of both management commit-tees and staff, while it may help avoid stagnation, makes management far more difficult than it would be in a local authority. Part of the problem arises from the idealistic and inexperienced nature of many of the staff, who see themselves as sacrificing all for the 'good of the cause'. Some voluntary groups seem prone to the most vicious internal struggles, which in turn can cause sponsors to lose interest.

6.9 Unrealistic objectives

The other side of pursuing multiple objectives is the tendency of voluntary groups to try to do too much all at once. This leads to internal conflicts and the failure to achieve results. Because of the idealism of the originators of a project, there can be a tendency to try to solve all the world's problems in one project. Lack of experience and an over-reliance on democracy can guarantee a group failing to achieve results, which in turn causes it to lose support. If realistic and attainable objectives are not specified, groups will fail to secure the grants they need to employ staff or extend their activities. In contrast, it is said that commercial businesses are far better at setting clear objectives, which lead to their success. However, most environmental projects would emphasise that they are trying to demonstrate an alternative system to the commercial world, rather than imitate it.

6.10 Fragmentation

The small size of most groups, and their grassroots origins, tends to lead to groups being isolated from each other. Groups often arise to meet a threat which leads them into conflict with authority. They are also often run by highly individualistic and militant people who attract publicity for themselves. As a result there is a tendency for authorities to dismiss voluntary groups as being too disorganised or duplicating each other, or as being unrepresentative. This is made worse by the tendency of many people in the voluntary sector to attack each other publicly. It has been observed in both Belgium and the UK that many groups stand outside the system of political parties. In turn, community groups in particular find it hard to convince authorities to back them, because they are seen as presenting too great a risk and too much of an administrative burden for the benefits they offer. Public agencies are concerned above all to avoid criticism for anything going wrong, and the worst crime of all is misappropriation of funds. In contrast, the more established national organisations are preferred as recipients of grants, even though they may lack the true strengths of voluntary action.

6.11 Amateurishness

The final criticism of voluntary groups is that they are amateurish in their approach, and that their standards are unacceptably low. This is not particularly fair as the voluntary groups are generally run by enthusiasts who are often specialists in their particular fields. The criticism tends to come from paid professional staff who have gone through extensive training programmes, and who resent voluntary competitors securing resources they would have liked or even worse getting all the publicity. Thus, a project to restore neglected Etruscan ruins in Italy ran first into lack of support and then into complete opposition from the local authority, who finally succeeded in closing the project down on the grounds of inadequate records. In practice, where groups are affected by such criticisms it is often because they have failed to rally local support. There is a danger that groups of enthusiastic, but inexperienced, volunteers 'parachute' on a community and promote a project that is not seen by local people as offering any benefits. If the project then succeeds in attracting public grants while local initiatives do not, it is not surprising that conflicts can erupt.

The tendency of voluntary groups to be started by people who are not professional is often the reason why they are able to pioneer and innovate. Indeed, if anyone was to work out the chances of success and all the obstacles, few would embark on setting up an environmental project. This makes some of the published books and guides on 'how to run a project' quite irrelevant, as pioneers prefer to go on doing things, rather than read manuals. However, because environmental projects depend on securing access to property and complying with planning and other regulations, a degree of professionalism is essential. Rather than concluding that community groups are not qualified to be involved in environmental projects, it is necessary to understand what leads to success, and how it can be replicated.

7   CONCLUSIONS

Though the environmental projects examined were concerned with very different objectives and situations, it is still possible to draw some general conclusions about what leads to success. These factors, which are all basically associated with the way the project is managed, offer some useful tips as far as both project selection and also the provision of assistance are concerned and the policy that should be adopted towards voluntary actions in the environment. While they are in no particular order of importance, they roughly correspond to the seven stages involved in going from the original vision to lasting results.

7.1 Finding the right driving force

It is the common experience of those involved in promoting new businesses that you cannot have ideas for other people. The crucial ingredient is always the individual who is determined enough to overcome all the hurdles. Some authorities make the mistake of putting the emphasis on evaluating the project, or the constitution, or even the resources available, whereas in reality it is the quality of the key individuals involved that matters most. This does not mean that voluntary projects require 'organisation men'. Indeed most entrepreneurs (both commercial and social) tend to be misfits, who seek to change the world rather than themselves. Such leaders can be found in the most surprising places (and a high proportion are women). The only generalisation is that probably they tend to lack formal qualifications, and that often they come from outside the community concerned. Sometimes the driving force can be a figure in authority who wants to try out a new idea (but this can lead to failure if the project does not respond to a felt community need). There are also many cases where unemployed professionals, such as landscape architects, take the initiative and build a group around themselves.

7.2 Forging a partnership between the community and authority

However militant a group might be to get started, it will need to win allies if it is ever to obtain control over resources. This means being able to compromise with authority so that the ideas and energy of the community group is backed up by the resources of the authority. Thus the Ironbridge Gorge Museums Trust owes much of its success to the fact that right at the beginning the Development Corporation for the area decided to back the project. Similarly the French Le Creusot project started with a subsidy from the French government. Partnerships involve more than legal structures and provision for representation. They involve communities being able to articulate their needs and work within some of the constraints under which public authorities operate. This requires great skills of diplomacy on the part of those running the project and a good deal of understanding and flexibility on the part of public authorities. It also often requires the use of public relations and marketing techniques, and a capacity to give sponsors more than their fair share of the credit!

7.3 Tapping professional expertise

In going from a set of loose objectives to a practical plan that can attract the resources needed for its implementation, some professional expertise is usually required. This includes legal skills in negotiating for land and securing approval for constitutions, architectural skills in designing schemes, surveying skills in preparing cost estimates, and accounting or financial skills in preparing budgets and grant applications. In short,

environmental groups who want to propose viable schemes need to understand the development management process, and how to put a 'deal' together.

The most successful groups either manage to attract members prepared to donate these skills, or else work with sympathetic professional firms. In some cases students at universities prove useful in working up schemes, and it is perhaps significant that many of the case studies came from towns with universities in them. In other cases, groups have managed to draw on the technical services of local authorities to work up their ideas. A new source of support, which is becoming increasingly important in the UK, is the use of community technical aid centres, that is non-profit intermediaries supported through government grants who provide free or subsidised technical advice to groups. There are a rapidly growing number of architects interested in practising what has been called 'community architecture', and this also applies to ecologists and landscape designers (though unfortunately not those involved with finance). Incidentally, it is wrong to suppose that expertise always resides in those who have had formal training. In many fields, such as community development or even canal restoration, it is first-hand practical experience that counts for most. Community groups interviewed often resented the tendency of so-called professionals to dismiss their practical experience because it was not backed up with qualifications.

7.4 Showing early results

Even where very ambitious schemes are involved, it is usually crucial to produce some early signs of achievement. These can be very small, such as clearing and fencing a waste site or they can involve a festival which brings a site to life for a short while. The important part is that those involved feel they have achieved something, so that they will be prepared to expend more time. Also 'nothing succeeds like success' and it is important to build a track record that overcomes scepticism.

A strategy is therefore required which involves a series of phases or stages, and where the first work can be done within the group's own resources. The transition from producing a paper plan to creating physical results is not only important for the self-esteem of the group but also has a major impact on authority and those who can provide resources. Often groups try to do too much all at once, and thus fail to achieve anything for all their effort. This is where well-thought out business or strategic planning is often needed.

7.5 Exploiting the media

An important aspect of securing access to site and producing results is the use of the media: newspapers, radio and television. The image of a project is very much created by the way it is reported. The most successful projects are often the ones that can best excite public interest. For example, schemes that involve children in planting trees help to win supporters among the unconverted. This includes projecting ideas, proposals and achievements and often means making the most of 'David and Goliath' struggles, between the community and public authorities. Environmental projects have to employ all the techniques of commercial enterprises in terms of marketing and public affairs. Indeed, they often seem better at using imagination to come up with remarkable logos and names. Imagination can also be applied to the way demonstrations are organised, so that public opinion is mobilised behind the project. A sympathetic journalist may be as important as having a financial expert on the committee! The Groundwork Trusts in the UK have been particularly successful, in effect acting as franchisees for a concept, rather like an environmental version of MacDonald's Hamburgers.

7.6 Having fun

Voluntary organisations cannot be on the attack all the time. However noble the aims, it is vital to retaining supporters that they enjoy the contribution they are asked to make. This means keeping volunteers informed and providing a variety of work. It also means organising celebrations that bring people together and make the most of any achievements. Festivals can be used to animate areas and to demonstrate their potential. They are also excellent ways of involving and rewarding sponsors through the provision of favourable publicity. Projects that complain of the work falling on too few shoulders often suffer from being too serious and self-righteous. Similarly, meetings that go on endlessly and with recriminations soon lead to all but the amateur politicians dropping out.   Many voluntary projects are concerned to demonstrate alternatives to the conventional way of doing things. They aim to practise participative management styles. Yet these can be difficult to make work, particularly if their hard-core activists are inexperienced and over earnest. Some people may dismiss community arts activities as amateurish or irrelevant. Yet if people feel better about themselves and each other, and develop a sense of pride, many of the other problems, such as isolation or vandalism, will start to go away.

7.7 Spreading the administrative load

The final problem, which is well-known in the voluntary sector, is the 'burning out' of key activists. The individuals driving the project take on too much and go on too long without respite, until they eventually collapse. The lack of compensation, the cost in terms of relationships, and the endless problems of tackling intractable problems with inadequate resources in a world which does not seem to care, can in time destroy the enthusiasm of the most able. One solution is to enable 'social entrepreneurs' to receive recognition, for example, by ending up as consultants or acknowledged experts.

While it is very difficult to turn entrepreneurs into professional managers, nevertheless the most successful projects are ones which have adapted to the changes required by growth. A good example in the UK is Pennine Heritage, which now effectively runs a multi-divisional business, ranging from building restoration to publishing. The key to success has been recruiting the right staff to run ongoing projects and focusing voluntary efforts on developing new areas of activity. Conversely, those projects that have pursued very narrow objectives, such as perhaps the amazing entomological society of Bielefeld in Germany, with 100 publications, 2,000 field trips, 800 work evenings, and which had identified 100 species of butterflies, not surprisingly felt over-loaded. The management burden can be spread by attracting in people who have taken early retirement but who still want to keep active. Early retirement and then involvement in community projects represents an important way of sharing work and coping with the problems of unemployment. These could also be eased by providing management training, which is very under-resourced at present. This is something which large organisations, both public and private, need to encourage.

7.8 Conclusions

Voluntary action has most to contribute in situations where there is a need to involve the community and to pursue a number of objectives simultaneously. It is also important as a source of innovation, while the low overheads and scope for job creation, make it of interest to the State. Voluntary action is also of public value because it taps the commitment of concerned individuals and provides a sense of fulfilment. It is sometimes a vital element in preserving freedom of expression and counteracting the dominance of big organisations. However many voluntary groups also suffer from vulnerability (particularly if a grant is stopped), unrealistic objectives, fragmentation, and are sometimes criticised for amateurishness.

To be successful therefore, as the previous chaper argued, projects need to find the right driving force, forge a partnership between the community and authority, tap professional expertise, show early results, exploit the media, have fun, and spread the administrative load. This is extremely difficult, but not impossible to do. It could be made much easier if government, local authorities and business were to provide more ongoing support in terms of both career development and training.

8 THE EUROPEAN DIMENSION

The diverse nature of environmental concerns - embracing the built environment, land use and natural resources - and the existing heavy pressures on European Community resources suggest at first that this should not be a matter which concerns the European Commission, however valuable the individual initiatives. But a review of the Community's existing concerns and new interests indicates that, in fact, voluntary work and the environment will be a growth area. This is because it cuts across a number of otherwise intractable problems (which are summarised in Chapter 3) and presents a source of hope, rather than a major problem, and one that should be encouraged rather than legislated for. The removal of obstacles to growth and the promotion of new forms of activity and cooperation run through much of the Commission's work. The Commission's concerns then are also likely to embrace the problems of abandoned buildings and wasteland, the creation of a civilised environment in which to live, work and play, and moves towards a sustainable economic base.

The private sector is often put off being involved by the high risks and availability of easier options elsewhere. Nor is it equipped to pursue projects with multiple objectives. Local government faces growing problems with declining resources. It too finds difficulty in mounting complex regeneration projects that involve the collaboration of many different actors. There is a possibility that voluntary action - the collaboration of people who care deeply about some common cause - in some cases will provide the crucial energy or driving force that is needed to overcome cynicism, inertia or despair. Certainly in the USA, where there has been far greater experimentation in dealing with these problems, great stress is placed on the use of 'non - profit' agencies, set up for the purpose of promoting development and working with all the existing 'stakeholders', or groups with an interest in the outcome. Vision and commitment are important qualities that are crucial to mobilisation of resources. The 'sweat equity' of individuals who have laboured away on a voluntary basis to get some environmental projects moving can be as valuable as the apparently well-worked out project proposal of the public agency.

8.1 Dissemination of good practice

Another important benefit from European collaboration is the chance to learn from other people who have tackled similar problems in different ways. The scale of the problems are too great for everyone to learn by their own mistakes. Already there are the beginnings of networks that operate on a European level. Publications like those of ELISE and the OECD on Local Employment Initiatives are seeking to spread good practice and put people in touch with each other. Networks, like the National Federation of City Farms and Community Gardens in the UK, have already had their first international meeting, and individual projects are now having visitors from other countries. The scope for innovation is immense, as individual countries have focussed on different types of problem. The 'pilot projects' being undertaken as part of an action research programme into local economic development by the European Social Fund provide an example of what needs to be done in the environmental field.

Reports such as the work by Volonteurope, and the study on Voluntary Work and Unemployment in four European countries by the Policies Studies Institute, have shown the potentially controversial nature of voluntary work. However, the case studies in this research have demonstrated that what might be called Local Environmental Development Initiatives are not replacing existing services with cheap labour. They are generally undertaking a crucial role that no-one else is prepared or able to take on in areas of real social need. Furthermore, these local initiatives are generally operating with the bare minimum of resources in terms of staff and funding, which limits their effectiveness. Because their activities are often pioneering, and may cut across different departmental boundaries, they find it difficult to secure the on-going support needed to maintain the interest of volunteers. Many go from crisis to crisis, and like small enterprises, never reach maturity. Only a few currently benefit from the technical assistance of qualified intermediaries, or receive any form of management training. The situation in terms of support also seems to vary greatly between different EC countries (though we have not been able to cover this fully within the resources available for this research study).

The case studies and the six national reports show that voluntary action in the environment deserves to be considered as a 'third force' in tackling environmental problems. In particular it is exceptionally well-suited to making good use of resources that are currently going to waste, such as unemployed people, vacant buildings and wasteland. Where major programmes consciously set out to respond to local concerns and to involve people in their solution, the evidence is that the results will be enhanced and appreciated more. For the regeneration of run-down areas requires far more than just money. It also depends on the people who live and work in the area forming a community in which people collaborate. This process, which enables individuals to develop to their full potential and feel a sense of pride in their neighbourhood, can be as important as conventional job creation measures in creating viable places. It will also lead to spin-offs in terms of new work in fields such as industrial tourism, environmental education, and landscape maintenance.

It would also help if the European Commission were to ensure that major Programmes, such as those supported by the European Regional Development Fund, had an explicit environmental dimension into which voluntary organisations could tap.

9   SUGGESTIONS FOR THE EUROPEAN COMMISSION

The suggestions in this report focus on practical steps that can be taken to encourage local initiatives that assist the implementation of European Community policies. The recommendations cover three types of action.

o   The first concerns recognition, so that local initiatives are taken more seriously (rather as small and medium-sized enterprises now are)

o   The second concerns funding, so that local initiatives that have gone beyond the stage of protest to playing a management or development role can secure funds to enable them to become self-sustaining

o   The third concerns technical assistance, and creating effective networks of intermediaries that can disseminate information, provide advice, and offer technical and managerial training

For each type of action, the role of the EC has first been highlighted, and then the implications for national and local governments are considered briefly.

9.1 Recognition

There is a need at the European level to recognise the role that local initiatives can play in programmes for economic, social and environmental regeneration. This is particularly important now that the Community provides such a major potential source of funds in the most run-down areas, and also because of the new stress on Integrated Operations Studies that link different programmes together. At present when voluntary organisations seek to promote development or set up businesses, they often run into opposition from both the public and private sectors. The Commission of the European Communities can help by ensuring that properly constituted development trusts are treated as if they formed part of the public sector in terms of, for example, eligibility for support from the European Regional Development Fund.

A similar, but possibly more difficult measure, would be to exempt non - profit or charitable organisations from having to pay Value Added Tax, which imposes an extra burden on voluntary organisations which they cannot usually recover. The Community could also help by drawing up or recognising model constitutions that could be adopted by local initiatives seeking recognition, possibly working through appropriate networks, like the National Federation of Community Associations in the UK and their equivalents in other members of the Community. There is also a need in some countries to ensure that insurance cover is available on acceptable terms for people involved in voluntary projects.

Another method of encouraging the growth of local initiatives is to spread information, and this report could be a useful first step. While there are many informal networks that occasionally bring people with a common interest together, most suffer from the lack of basic resources to cover administration and travel. There is a strong case for national governments to grant-aid associations that bring together local groups to share experience and develop expertise. If this is not to be confined to the better-off, it is important that funds are available to cover membership, either through direct support to associations or by making this a part of any grant application. Such associations can play a similar role to trade associations in the business world, and are an essential element in overcoming the criticisms of amateurishness that are sometimes made.

9.2 Funding

While there is a case for funding some pilot or demonstration projects, the EC is too far removed from local situations to be generally involved in funding voluntary initiatives. However, there is a strong case for ensuring that programmes funded through Integrated Operations Studies make some specific allowance for supporting the growth of local environmental initiatives in the area. This would cover making funds available to groups who will take over and manage some of the land that is improved under a major land reclamation scheme, and then involve local people in its use, for example in growing vegetables. There is a need for funding for demonstration projects aimed at transferring experience between countries, using feasibility studies to help package finance together from different public sources. A European Community initiative in this area would certainly be useful.

For many people, the major function of the European Community is to concentrate resources on a scale that is larger than individual communities can muster. This helps to explain the major investments being made in infrastructure with European funding, including projects with mainly environmental objectives. The need for the mobilisation of large-scale resources applies wherever the project is intrinsically big in relation to the scale of the authorities concerned. This includes projects that cross authority boundaries, like the restoration of an old canal, for example. It also could include major groups of buildings of international importance, that are of a size that cannot be coped with locally. The conservation of some of the very large textile mills would come into this category. At the moment, the conservation of historic buildings and monuments has very limited public funds at its disposal, and these have often gone in the past on buildings associated with the very rich, such as country mansion houses. Industrial decline has now put a new priority on the industrial heritage, without making any extra resources available. Schemes such as those by Pennine Heritage in England, and for Le Creusot in France, illustrate the scope for beginning the difficult process of regenerating run-down areas by starting with their heritage. Few other possibilities exist for creating work on such a large scale so rapidly. Rather than spreading available resources very thinly, there is a strong case for focussing some of the European Regional Development Fund on area regeneration schemes for sites that need help to avoid unique resources being lost for ever.

While most progress is likely to be made by redirecting mainstream programmes and budgets, there may also be a case for enlarging the European Heritage Fund. The idea would be to support major local initiatives that involve the industrial heritage, and that require very substantial public investment before private investment can be attracted. It is clear from the case studies that some local environmental development initiatives are trying to rescue areas or buildings that form part of Europe's cultural heritage. The resources required far outstrip local capacity. Examples include the restoration of some of the historic textile mills and canals that date from the start of the industrial revolution, and some industrial neighbourhoods in major cities. There is a case for going beyond awards, and setting up a fund to provide a mixture of grants and soft loans for major regeneration schemes that seek to transform the future of run-down areas that have buildings of architectural significance at the European level. This might also seek to mobilise private funds through tax incentives, and investigations are needed in each country into the implications. There may also need to be a national clearing house to ensure resources are directed where they are most needed, and not to improving the environment of those who are already well off.

If voluntary action is to play a larger role on a continuing basis, then sources of funds are needed to cover the core running costs. These include salaries for administrators, and for volunteer organisers, as well as funds for premises and promotion. One way this can be achieved is for designated management posts to be created within voluntary groups for purposes such as coordinating the work of volunteers and running job creation programmes. These can then be funded by national governments under short-term contracts for periods of say 3-5 years.

In many areas where investment is needed, there will be associations who are trying to improve conditions. Instead of public agencies 'parachuting' on an area, and organising improvements, there are considerable merits in taking the extra time to work with local initiatives, whether these be organised around ethnic groups or special interests. By giving local initiatives a positive role to play, not only will communications be improved, and programmes made more relevant, but the wider aims of development will also be secured, thus ensuring that any physical improvements are maintained and appreciated.

One method for ensuring the survival of local initiatives is for voluntary groups to enter into medium-term service contracts with local authorities to provide and run certain environmental services that contribute to education, recreation or even economic

development. This could be a requirement in programmes that are financially supported by the European Community. Further research is needed into the job creation
effects that could flow from directing more Community resources through the voluntary
sector.

9.3 Technical assistance

The final recommendation arises out of the need to spread experience so that under-
resourced groups do not have to 're-invent the wheel'. Most people seem to agree that
the best source of advice is to discuss proposals with people who have done something
similar before. Hence, there is great value in enabling 'social entrepreneurs' to visit
other projects. This could be achieved through a system of European travel fellowships
which would enable people who were planning major projects to visit 'model' projects in
other countries. There is scope for international companies like airlines or computer
companies also sponsoring such an approach which might be run through networks or
linked to training courses.

It is no use providing more money if groups lack the managerial or technical expertise
to use resources productively. On the whole, voluntary initiatives use limited resources
very efficiently, but problems can arise when they grow rapidly or tackle unfamiliar
tasks. Two solutions seem worth developing more widely. The first is the provision of
community technical aid centres, which make available architectural expertise, design
and often accounting and other skills to community groups in major urban connurba-
tions. The British model, where the Department of the Environment provides support
through an Urban Initiatives Fund, could be replicated elsewhere in Europe. But there
is also a need to tap other sources of funds, and here again tax incentives could be used
to encourage private individuals and companies to channel resources to local initiatives
through technical aid centres.

The second approach is to provide training in project management for both paid staff and voluntary management committees. There are already good precedents in France and Italy for using the educational system to support the growth of 'green' initiatives. However, there is also a need to improve management in the voluntary sector. Support for environmental management training would be an effective way both of raising standards and of disseminating experience across national boundaries. This could include the production of simple handbooks, as well as free guides to sources of information and assistance. The Social Fund already supports innovative training schemes and has funded at least one training scheme for environmental managers. This is something which deserves serious consideration at the European level in order to bring together different training schemes in a coordinated way.

In conclusion, within the limited resources of what is inevitably a pioneering study, some light has hopefully been shed on what could emerge as a major 'third force' in tackling the problems of the post-industrial revolution and creating a new renaissance in and around our cities.

LIST OF NATIONAL REPORTS AND CASE STUDIES

Belgium

Miller, J., Delruelle-Vosswinkel, N., Initiatives Linked to Voluntary Work in the Environment, Institute of Sociology, Free University of Brussels, 1986

Case studies:

-   Arlon - Revival of the Upper City
    (Arlon - Renaissance du Haut de la Ville)
-   The Association of the Central Canal
    (Compagnie du Canal du Centre)
-   Urban Research and Action Workshop
    (Atelier de Recherche et d'Action Urbaines (ARAU))
-   Working Party of Les Marolles
    (Comité Général d'Action des Marolles)
-   Hellegat and Rupel-Enviornment Groups
    (Groupes Hellegat et Rupel-Environnement)
-   Liège - District Improvement Competition (summary)
    (Liège - Concours "Qualité-Quartiers")
-   Charleroi-Environment (summary)
    (Charleroi-Environnement)
-   "The Prairie" City Farm Project (summary)
    (Mouscron - La Prairie)
-   The Soignes Forest Heritage Association (summary)
    (Les Amis de la Forêt de Soignes)
-   Brussels - Standing Inventory of Vacant Industrial Premises (summary)
    (Bruxelles - Inventaire permanent des locaux industriels vacants)
-   Ghent - Community Centres (summary)
    (Gand - Les maisons de quartier)

France

Legru, B., Initiatives Linked to Voluntary Work in the Environment, SEEDA, Paris, 1986

Case studies:

- The Ecological Garden, Promenade du Préfet
  (Le Jardin Ecologique "Promenade du Préfet")
- Converting a municipal tip - Nature Club of Bailleul
  (L'aménagement d'une décharge municipale)
- Building garages, Lyon
  (L'auto-construction de garages)
- The Nature and Environment Group at la Chapelle-sur-Erdre, Nantes
  (Le Groupe Nature Environnement)
- FIR-Lorraine - Educational Centre for the Discovery of Nature
  (Le Centre Pédagogique de Découverte de la Nature)
- Waters and Rivers of Brittany
  (Eaux et Rivières de Bretagne)
- Community Association for the Development of Industrial Tourism at
  Creusot-Montceau-les-Mines
  (L'Association Communautaire de Développement du Tourisme Industriel
  de Creusot-Montceau-les-Mines)

Germany

Noeke, J., Lossin, B., Toennes, A., "Citizens' initiatives" in the environment: a study of voluntary and unpaid work in the environment, Institut für Umweltschutz an der Universität Dortmund, 1986

Case studies:

- Alliance for the Environment and Nature Protection in Germany, Hagen District Branch
  (Bund für Umwelt und Naturschutz Deutschland e.V. (BUND), Kreisgruppe Hagen)
- Rein-Berg Nature Protection Association
  (Rheinisch-Bergischer Naturschutzverein (RBN) e.V.)
- Association for the Protection of Germany's Forests and the League of Young Germans for the Protection of Forests, Ringelstein Branch
  (Schutzgemeinschaft Deutscher Wald (SDW) und Deutsche Waldjugend Ringelstein)
- Working Party of Entomologists of East Westphalia and Lippe
  (Arbeitsgemeinschaft ostwestfälisch-lippischer Entomologen e.V.)
- Working Party for the Protection of Amphibians and Reptiles in Dortmund
  (Arbeitsgemeinschaft Amphibien-und Reptilienschutz Dortmund (AGARD))
- Women's Organisation of Planners and Architects
  (Feministische Organisation von Planerinnen und Architektinnen Dortmund e.V.)
- Society for the Promotion of Democratic Town Planning - the Planners Workshop
  (Verein zur Förderung demokratischer Stadtplanung e.V. - Planerladen)
- Detmold Citizens' Urban Renewal Campaign
  (Bürgeraktion Stadtsanierung Detmold e.V.)
- Dortmund Producers' and Consumers' Community
  (Erzeuger und Verbraucher Gemeinschaft Dortmund)

Italy

Depaoli, P., Fatello, M., Lombardo, S., Truffi, C., Initiatives Linked to Voluntary Work in the Environment, ARPES s.r.l., Rome, 1986

Case studies:

- Woodland in the City - Italia Nostra, Milan Section
  (Bosco in città, Italia Nostra, Sez. Milano)
- The Green University
  (Università Verde)
- Collection of used electric batteries - World Wildlife Fund (WWF) Italy
  (Raccolta pile elettriche usata)
- Museum of Farming Civilization - "Oxbell Group"
  (Museo della civiltà contadina -Gruppo della Studura)
- Restoration of the Way of the Underworld - Rome Archaeological Group
  (Recupero della Via degli Inferi - Gruppo Archeologico Romano (GAR))
- Archaeological cooperative
  (Cooperativa Archeologia)
- Rehabilitation of the Lake of Martignano
  (Salvaguardia Lago di Martignano)
- Renovation of the "Rocks" of Matera - La Scaletta Circle
  (Recupero dei "sassi" di Matera - Circolo La Scaletta)

The Netherlands

Van der Linden, J. W., Local Initiatives Linked to Voluntary Work in the Environment, Institute for Environmental Studies, Free University of Amsterdam, 1986

Case studies:

- Garbage dump restored to nature area
  (Stortplaats wordt weer natuurgebied)
- The improvement of the Overschie Lakes Area and the De Tempel Country Estate
  (De verbetering van het Overschiese Plassengebied in het landgoed de Tempel)
- Nature conservation in a new residential area: the Lunetten Greenery Group, Utrecht
  (Natuurbescherming in een nieuwbouwwijk: de Groengroep Lunetten)
- The "De Kiem" neighbourhood farm
  (Buurtboerderij De Kiem)
- The Ecological Cycle Foundation, Arnhem
  (De Ecologische Kringloop Stichting)
- The "De Watermolen" Visitors' Centre in Arnhem
  (Bezoekerscentrum De Watermolen in Arnhem)
- The Nieuw-Waldeck district garden
  (De Wijktuin Nieuw-Waldeck)
- Volunteers preserve a characteristic landscape
  (Vrijwilligers behouden een karakteristiek landschap)

United Kingdom

Davidson, J., Initiatives Linked to Voluntary Work in the Environment, Barlett School of Architecture and Planning, University College London, 1986

Case studies:

- Ashram Acres, Birmingham
- Windmill Hill City Farm, Bristol
- Benwell Nature Park, Newcastle
- Oldham and Rochdale Groundwork Trust
- Thrum Hall Nature Area
- Sholver Rangers
- Rochdale Canal
- Pennine Heritage, Hebden Bridge
- Blists Hill, Ironbridge Gorge Museum
- Wirksworth, Derbyshire
- Provost Estate, London
- Community Support Anti-Waste Scheme, Cardiff

SUMMARY OF SELECTED CASE STUDIES

B.1 Belgium: Working Party of Les Marolles, Brussels (CGAM)

B.2 Belgium: Association of the Central Canal, Wallonia

B.3 France: Community Association for the Development of Industrial Tourism, Le Creusot-Montceau-les-Mines

B.4 Germany: Working Party for the Protection of Amphibians and Reptiles in Dortmund (AGARD)

B.5 Germany: Women's Organisation of Planners and Architects, (FOPA)

B.6 Italy: Woodland in the City, Milan

B.7 The Netherlands: The Ecological Cycle Foundation, Arnhem (EKS)

B.8 The Netherlands: The Lunetten Greenery Group Utrecht

B.9 UK: Pennine Heritage, Hebden Bridge

B.10 UK: Windmill Hill City Farm, Bristol

B.1

BELGIUM: Working Party of des Marolles, Brussels (CGAM)

In l969 the Working Party of Les Marolles (CGAM) was formed to fight redevelopment in an inner city area of Brussels. Les Marolles district covers an area of some 50 hectares in the centre of Brussels. The authorities consider it 'uninhabitable', with run-down blocks of flats, overcrowding and unsanitary conditions. Les Marolles has always played a role as a reception area for immigrants into Brussels, and has a high concentration of disadvantaged people. In fact, throughout its history there has been a strong sense of solidarity and community among the multi-racial population. In 1969 part of the district was put under a compulsory purchase order and residents reacted with the creation of CGAM, swiftly achieving their first objective of making the state give up its plans and, in addition, set up a 'pilot' renovation programme for the district.

CGAM has been a pioneer in the sphere of urban renewal, the fight to improve housing conditions for the most deprived and the creation of community businesses. 'Les Marolles Renovation Working Party' has been responsible for the construction of 171 domestic dwellings and 4 business premises, as well as the refurbishment of 28 homes and the Youth Centre. The 'Marolles Commission', set up in 1984, has liaised with the authorities to improve streets and squares and provide playgrounds and trees. The 'Marolles Development Company', an offshoot of CGAM concerned with the economic development of the district, has launched several mini-enterprises including a workshop or recycling television sets and an office-cleaning company. Other CGAM initiatives linked to the environment have included increasing residents' involvement in the rehabilitation of the district, and, in conjunction with the City authorities, the creation of an urban farm for local children.

CGAM is administered by a voluntary Board of Management which reports to a General Meeting of the 50 or so voluntary members. The members often join when a problem concerns them directly but have been harder to keep on a long-term basis. Funding has depended on the variable support of successive regional authorities and the EEC.

Delays in payment have forced CGAM to take out bank loans and to attempt to cover interest costs by obtaining donations from individuals and associations.

As a result of CGAM's initiative, there has been a great physical improvement in the district which has been preserved as a traditional quarter of Brussels. In the long-term CGAM seeks to make progress equally on social, economic and cultural fronts.

B.2

BELGIUM: Association of the Central Canal, Wallonia

The Compagnie du Canal du Centre was founded in 1977 following the experience of a teacher visiting the Ironbridge Gorge Museum of industrial archaeology in England, and then sailing through the heart of the Black Country on traditional narrow boats. Coming down through the Anderton lift, engineers explained its history and the links with Belgium and France. On returning to Belgium, he learned that a 1,350 tonne canal was planned to replace the old Canal du Centre (380 tonnes) and that the four lifts would be replaced by a single electrically operated funicular lift.

In most cases, industrial archaeology comes after the abandonment and often the partial destruction, of a site. The situation of the Canal du Centre was unique. The region is part of the industrial centre of Wallonia which, apart from one remaining iron and steel works and a few cement works, had become an economic wasteland. However, the canal was still a commercially used navigable waterway and already a major site of industrial archaeology. It offered an exceptional opportunity for action: the old lifts still had at least 10 years to go before being replaced by the new lift. A non-profit-making association was therefore set up to take all steps to ensure the full and active protection of the Canal du Centre, including its lifts and lock-keepers' houses, while making this unique heritage publicly available through wide-ranging cultural and educational activities.

The association initially organised an exhibition to attract public attention to the international historic importance of the canal and its value as part of the architectural heritage. It contacted the Ministry of Public Works which manages the canal, and which let them have a series of lock-keepers' houses for token rents on condition that they were renovated. Another non-profit-making association, the Centre d'Animation en Langues (Language Promotion Centre), run by the same person and which organises language courses on commuter trains, gave financial help to fund the purchase of a boat for excursions. The revenue from the first trips made it possible to begin renovation work on the lock-keepers' houses. Five disused lock-keepers' houses were ultimately renovated and converted for re-use including a museum, offices, and an exhibition room.

Four prizes awarded to the association during 1984 and 1985 brought the initiative increased publicity and considerable funds, in addition to funds from the Centre d'Animation en Langues and occasional grants from the French Community Ministry. Most revenue comes, however, from visitors: 3,600 in 1984, 10,000 in 1985 and 20,000 anticipated in 1986. The association has also received support in the form of facilities or materials from the Commune of Thieu, the local iron and steel works and the Belgium railway company.

At the outset the initiative was run entirely by volunteers including the promoter who is a teachers' training college lecturer, his students who helped with the restoration of the first lock-keeper's house and a canal transport expert. From 1980 staff were contracted by the Ministry for short periods, many with specialist expertise such as mechanical engineering and graphic design. Before and after their contract periods, many were able to work for the association while drawing unemployment benefit.

The initiative has achieved significant results in protecting the heritage and also has economic and social dimensions since the rehabilitation of the canal is likely to affect the tourist development of the region and will offer the young and underprivileged employment.

B.3

FRANCE: Community Association for the Development of Industrial Tourism, Le Creusot-Montceau-les-Mines

The Community Association for the Development of Industrial Tourism is concerned with the industrial sites in Le Creusot-Montceau-les-Mines, an area of with almost 110,000 inhabitants whose main employment has traditionally been in the iron and steel industry. Its objective is to organise discovery trails revealing the history of local industrial development since the end of the 18th century, including visits to museums, as well as presenting current economic activities by means of visits to companies and debates or symposia. In 1985 the Association organised about 100 trips. It has since been contacted by other bodies elsewhere in France, for example, Franche-Comté and Lorraine, who want to pursue similar projects.

The project was originally devised and drawn up by a committed individual with the assistance of Le Creusot Promotion Association, which agreed to place its resources at his disposal. It was subsequently set up by two paid staff and brings together volunteers who previously worked in local industries. About 30 active members, who have taken early retirement or are pensioners, have been trained as guides leading trips of one or more days. Training events and courses are organised for new members and to bring guides' knowledge up-to-date. These also help members regain a sense of social identity. Various professionals and heads of companies concerned with tourist development are involved in order to optimise the economic effects of tourism and promote the region's image.

The association has three boards, one of about 40 active members who have trained as guides, one of de facto members, representing financiers and representatives of the local and regional authorities, and one of associated members who are representatives of bodies involved with the work of the associations. Active members are not paid for their work, and revenue from the trips is ploughed back into the association.

Following economic difficulties, many employees in local industries had been retired early and, as a result, Le Creusot was hard hit by unemployment. From the outset Le Creusot's local Council saw the development of the heritage industry as contributing to the community's revitalisation. The project was a national experiment and received exceptional initial funding including considerable support from government departments (of Employment, Tourism, Culture and Leisure) as well as local and regional authorities. In 1985 the state subsidies continued while revenue generated by the association grew. The aim of the association is to increase its volume of business so that it becomes completely self-financing.

B.4

GERMANY: Working Party for the Protection of Amphibians and Reptiles in Dortmund (AGARD)

In 1981 AGARD was founded as a Working Party of DGHT (German Herpetological and Terrariatological Association) by a policeman who felt that the Dortmund branch of DGHT did not show sufficient interest in local species. The Working Party's aim was to preserve the frogs, toads and newts in Dortmund's only nature reserve, which were liable to be destroyed in large numbers in the wake of construction and road improvement schemes. By 1983 AGARD had grown from a small group organised on an ad hoc basis to become an independent nature protection group extending its activities to the whole urban area of Dortmund. It has taken as its objective the protection and preservation of frogs, toads, newts, salamanders, lizards, slow-worms and snakes in the remaining open spaces in Dortmund.

AGARD currently has 250 members, of whom 80 to 100 regularly play an active part. Their ages range from 6 to 60 and about half are female. Many occupational groups are represented, from manual workers to doctors of technology, as well as teachers, professionals, students and schoolchildren. Following a suggestion by the city's Youth Office young people at risk are seconded onto AGARD projects and financial aid is received for this. There are wide variations in members' as knowledge, as some have been familiar with the work for years, while newcomers may have only a fundamental grounding. For some, AGARD has provided a springboard for a splendid, although unremunerative, career in nature protection in Dortmund.

There are four groups within the city, each covering an area of 20-30 km2, and made up of between 10 and 20 members. Each group includes specialists who can design leaflets and posters and can prepare slides. The four group controllers co-ordinate activities, maintain telephone communication and manage finance and public relations. Members are used within their locality and according to their inclinations and abilities. The telephone link between groups enables some 30 members to be called up within an hour to protect toads on the move. Activities have included creating new water courses, managing ponds and biotopes, setting up information stands, calling on officials and public lectures.

Funds come from donations by other nature protection associations or private individuals, usually members. The principal outlay is on postage and office supplies. The cost of telephone and photography, as well as equipment such as torches, is borne by members. The City authorities have paid for various items of equipment and materials.

AGARD gets excellent coverage in the media, in particular in Dortmund's three major newspapers. Over the years, its public image has become that of a busy nature protection association that does serious work, and it is viewed benevolently in political circles. Its greatest merit is seen as enhancing awareness of nature protection issues among Dortmund's population. However, any project is blocked if it competes with town planning. This means that, while nearly every pond within the municipal area is given into AGARD's care, it cannot prevent roads being built alongside.

B.5

GERMANY: Women's Organisation of Planners and Architects (FOPA)

FOPA was founded in 1981, in Berlin, to promote the needs of women in the city. Some of its members came from a recently formed group of women planners in Dortmund who subsequently founded FOPA Dortmund with the objective of promoting ecological and social improvements in the urban environment. In addition, there was concern to create jobs for female planners.

FOPA Dortmund has initiated projects in the western part of central Dortmund to re-establish the city's 'natural' cycle and to encourage others to do the same. Projects have included greening courtyards, recycling organic waste, creating a 'mothers' centre' and organising courses on ecological issues.

To encourage the participation of women in planning and improving their environment, emphasis was placed on up-grading the courtyards of residential blocks of flats to provide pleasant places for people to meet socially. In the Westpark district of Dortmund, the courtyards of residential blocks have a particular significance as there are very few other open spaces. However, most of them are ecological deserts, covered in concrete, walled up into small areas, and barely usable as playgrounds or for recreation and leisure. A survey was conducted which showed that most of the courtyards were used to store rubbish bins or bicycles, or were not used at all. Most residents were prepared to help actively in the re-creation of the yards. A programme of planting and installing leisure rooms brought nature back into the city and improved the quality of life for women residents.

Residents' were also willing to take part in an experiment to recycle organic domestic refuse via specially bred earthworms into fertiliser which is then supplied back to the households, or is used for the greening project initiated by FOPA Dortmund. Practical initiatives are backed up by intensive public relations, a touring exhibition and various lecture courses.

FOPA Dortmund has about 40 members, whose ages range from 20 to 40 years. A core of about 10 are actively involved in projects. Regular meetings are held where specific topics are discussed and action is planned. The Dortmund group co-operates with FOPA Berlin, exchanging ideas and experience, and in the production of a periodical. There is also contact with groups of women planners in Kassel and Hamburg.

While the work of the earlier group had been informally organised and mainly voluntary, with the foundation of FOPA Dortmund in 1985 it was felt that permanent jobs should be created for members, and that this would give more impetus and authority to their initiative. Finance is critical, mainly coming form members' donations and membership fees. Individual members have received grants under the government's job creation scheme, which has also provided the labour force for projects.

B.6

ITALY: Woodland in the City, Milan

In 1974 members of Italia Nostra, the Italian nature conservation association, identified the Cascina (or farm) of San Romano outside Milan as an area suitable for environmental restoration. It comprises about 25 hectares of land belonging to the municipality of Milan, originally settled in the 16th century to farm wheat and rye and with a small wood at its centre. In 1974, the farms leasing the land were not doing well and Italia Nostra approached the Municipality to entrust them with the area's management. Their aim was to create an open green space 'with urban characteristics and a natural content' that would be a pleasure to visit and would also benefit the City's ecosystem.

Italia Nostra's central nucleus is formed by about 10 people, 3 of whom are paid staff of the 'Woodland in the City' project. A team of experts, including a forestry expert, a landscape architect and a town planner, was involved from its earliest stages. An essential aspect of environmental work with volunteers was found to be the availability of experts to help prepare plans and to supervise work. Several thousand volunteers have taken part in the initiative, attracted through local media and leaflet drops in Milan. From 1975 to 1977, between 3-4,000 were involved and were joined by 8,000 schoolchildren as well as members of local Scout groups. Volunteers were mainly students seeking useful and sociable leisure activities, or unemployed, many of whom were looking for a first job. The volunteers' first task was creating woodland, after which a network of walks was laid out for visitors 'to enjoy and discover the area'.

Of the 35 hectares, three-quarters were fairly densely planted with species that had flourished in the Po Valley up until two or three centuries previously. This contains rich ornithological fauna including tits, red woodpeckers and owls, and provides a habitat for animals seeking food and safety near towns. The remaining quarter was laid out as open land around the 16th century farm, which was also restored. The farm is the main focus of public activity since there is no conventional playground.

This type of 'town park' was considered a model for nature conservation, costing a fraction of pure woodland restoration. Also the work could involve far more volunteers than, for example, buildings restoration. The original proposal was seen by the volunteers as a challenge to prove to the Municipality that environmental and nature conservation were possible. Relations with local institutions and specifically with the Municipality have developed well. The project's success is acknowledged and, having raised initial capital, a public subsidy of several million lire was subsequently given.

B.7

THE NETHERLANDS: The Ecological Cycle Foundation, Arnhem (EKS)

In 1981 Stefan Triest and Hans de Graaf set up as farmers in Arnhem, feeding their stock on vegetable peelings. Their request for a subsidy from the Municipality, equal to the cost of waste disposal, was unsuccessful. However, following publicity, the Institute for Waste Reprocessing offered a small grant for the collection of peelings over one year, making it possible for Stefan and Hans set up the Ecological Cycle Foundation, and invest in pails and a horse and cart as means of transport.

The Foundation collects kitchen waste, clothing and all kinds of domestic articles including furniture, television sets, refrigerators, stoves, bicycles and books. Organic waste is then sold as cattle fodder to local farmers, and the other articles are sold through the Foundation's two shops or to dealers. In 1983 the Foundation hired an old school building, part of which was used as workshops where repairs could be carried out on bicycles and electrical appliances. So as not to compete with businesses depending on repair work, the only articles repaired were those salvaged from domestic waste.

After about five years the Foundation had still not been given any real municipal support and sought publicity in various ways including trips to the Hague by horse and cart. Ultimately the European Social Fund and Arnhem's Municipal Council, aware that many residents supported the project, made funds available. As a result a training plan was drawn up and the 'Reuse Bureau', a commercial advice bureau was established to give information to other groups forming centres throughout the Netherlands, basing their approach on the Foundation's experience. In time the Foundation has received a number of subsidies from government departments also, but these have never been sufficient to acquire means of transport adequate to extend its activities.

Originally run as a form of workers' self-management, with increasing numbers of collaborators, the Foundation set up a central consultancy with representatives from the peeling collectors, shops and workshops bearing responsibility for day-to-day activities. Three teams each collect about 3 tonnes of waste daily. Local residents' collaboration is gained by lectures and leafletting households. Buckets are then delivered to each house, and collection is by horse and cart, which provides entertainment and amusement. In 1986 about 25 people were working on the project, some volunteers, some working out community service and a few paid labour. Equipment included three tractors, a lorry, a bus, four carts, carriers and containers, as well as about 40,000 pails.

The project was given the form of a Foundation so that others could also be involved. The unemployed could collaborate without losing their benefit. Those who want to develop ideas have the opportunity to try them out, and gradually the Foundation has attracted people otherwise unable to find suitable work. It acquired importance as an outlet for younger people from marginal groups. Many have alcohol or drugs problems or criminal records, and have been assigned to the Foundation as a form of community service. Some continued as volunteers after their period of service. For many of them, the project has offered the possibility of doing something that is valued and through which they can experience a sense of achievement.

B.8

NETHERLANDS: The Lunetten Greenery Group, Utrecht

Lunetten is a new residential district in Utrecht, developed to conserve some of the existing landscape features. In 1979, concerned about the maintenance of greenery by the Municipal Parks Departments, one of the residents founded the Lunetten Greenery Group. Members of the group tackled various 'restoration' jobs to conserve threatened landscape elements, including the willows and an orchard. They then carried out maintenance work on the parks, in the absence of any management plan.

With the increase in active members, new initiatives were evolved and general working parties were established to cover management of green spaces, including dykes and watercourses, maintenance of pollarded willows and meadow vegetation, providing nesting boxes to compensate for the loss of natural nesting sites as a result of building construction, and organising educational and publicity activities. Under the group's influence, more varied vegetation has been planted and a public 'home park' is being developed. Agreements are made with the municipality for each project.

The activities are co-ordinated by a management committee. There are 40-50 members of whom about 30 are active and a list of volunteers is drawn on for participation in particular projects. A number of biologists joined the group and contacts were made with experts in vegetation management from the Agricultural High School in Wageningen.

Funding comes from members' subscriptions and the group receives a small subsidy from the Lunetten Welfare Foundation, in addition to various incidental subsidies. The Foundation for Landscape Management makes implements available.

B.9

UK: Pennine Heritage, Hebden Bridge

In the 1970s various local societies in the South Pennines area, concerned about the loss of people and investment following the decline of the once important local cotton and woollen textile industries, came together to form the Pennines Park Association. They organised a major conference to discuss the potential for recreation and tourism and, to match these voluntary initiatives, local authorities set up the Standing Conference of South Pennines authorities as a discussion forum.

Practical action began with an initiative by three residents to save Birchcliffe Chapel from demolition. In 1979 they established Pennine Heritage Ltd as a charity based in the Chapel, 'to aid the social and economic regeneration of the Pennine communities'. Its five main aims are 'to strengthen Pennine identity through social, cultural and recreational activity; to create a better understanding of the area through information, advice and education; to assist the economic life of the area through the provision of workspace by the re-use of redundant historic buildings; to work closely with other organisations with similar interests; and to help preserve and develop the surrounding countryside.'

To meet these aims, Pennine Heritage developed a number of projects, concentrating on restoring buildings and publicising the special character of the area. The first major project was the development of the Birchcliffe Centre, restored to provide office and conference facilities, as well as a residential hostel. Subsequent projects included converting a 35,000 sq. ft mill in Hebden Bridge into workspace for small firms with the help of specialist volunteers. Queen Street Mill was restored jointly with Burnley District Council to provide workspace as well as a working cotton mill intended to generate income from both sales and visitors. Plans for the restoration of Clegg Hall, a Jacobean manor house, given to Pennine Heritage by a private benefactor, have prompted the designation of a surrounding Conservation Area and triggered local authority interest in protecting other buildings and creating a management trust for the area.

There is also the bi-monthly **Pennine Magazine**, that promotes the identity of the South Pennines area, publications on the geology, history and socio-economic development of the area and residential courses.

In addition, an Environmental Task Force provides work for local unemployed under government schemes, sometimes linking with other voluntary organisations, and undertaking a range of jobs for local authorities, landowners and public bodies, including drystone-walling, footpath clearance and maintenance, tree-planting and habitat conservation. In 1985 a marketing manager was appointed to try and raise local awareness of the work of Pennine heritage in part through Operation Merlin which draws on the resources of the Oral History Unit (an archive for the area) and the Environmental Task Force and includes gardening, talks and trips to local canals, railways and museums.

Major funders have been the Department of the Environment, Manpower Services Commission, the English Tourist Board, the Countryside Commission, English Heritage, the Architectural Heritage Fund, the Pilgrim Trust, the Carnegie UK Trust, the Joseph Rowntree Social Services Trust, local authorities and the EEC, and there have been some private donations. Annual turnover is over £1 million. Most of the income is derived from the sale of publications and bookings for the Birchcliffe Centre.

About 100 volunteers participate as members of project working parties and of the 15-strong Council of Management. They identify with the regeneration objectives of Pennine Heritage, but they are also concerned with achieving personal goals such as protecting a woodland or restoring a mill. Pennine Heritage would like to extend the opportunities for volunteers to do practical work, but the emphasis has been upon using the professional skills of trained and experienced volunteers in the working parties and on the Council of Management rather than providing opportunities for interested but non-professional people to be involved. Practical action is carried out by contract labour and as government employment training schemes.

B.10

UK: Windmill Hill City Farm, Bristol

In the spring of 1976, a group of local residents in Bedminster, South Bristol, objected to the City Council's proposal to use a Council-owned scrapyard on Windmill Hill as a high security lorry park. At an event organised to gauge local opinion, the idea of a city farm emerged and the Council agreed to lease the land at a peppercorn rent for five years. The aim was to 'provide a wide range of educational and recreational facilities for all groups in the community, and at the same time create an attractive, useful and productive environment.'

Volunteers began work in 1977, clearing the site, renovating a derelict building for workshops and meeting space, and establishing the farmyard. The first management committee was formed with local people and the farm was registered as a charity. It began raising funds from trusts and local companies, and canvassed for donations of materials. Grants under the government's Urban Programme provided the capital to establish the farm, pay for a full-time farmer and administrative staff and for building materials and equipment. The City Council gave grant aid to subsidise staff costs, increasingly paid for from the revenue of the farm's businesses. Avon County Council pays for staff to organise activities for the mentally-disturbed and elderly.

The site covers 4½ acres and has six main activity areas: farmyard (with play centre, workshops, craft and administration space, cafe and dairy), community gardens, grazing paddocks, chicken tractor system (for egg production), all-weather sports pitch, and a nature reserve. Responding to local needs, the farm's first community activity was a summer playscheme for children. A major achievement was a community bus service, organised with local councils and on a steep and narrow route that had been considered impossible. Other activities include a programme of 'community care', including parent support and youth counselling, and activities for the elderly. New demands, for example accessible gardens for the disabled and elderly, are continually being catered for.

Some 500 volunteers are associated with the farm, working alongside paid staff on practical tasks. Most volunteers are local, from all social groups. Some want experience while looking for paid work, others want to work with animals, or are seeking companionship. In addition, long-stay patients from a psychiatric hospital come to work, and during the farm's development a number of job creation programmes were funded by the government's Manpower Services Commission.

There is no overall director. Local volunteers serve on the Management Committee and there are sub-committees for finance and personnel and support groups for events and publicity. Training for staff and volunteers takes place on and off the farm, and some technical courses organised by the National Federation of City Farms take place at Windmill Hill, where the Federation's office is based.

In an area of high unemployment with few other community facilities, the farm offers something for everyone. Within ten years it transformed the area from a rubble landscape to a thriving community centre. Good links have been established with a network of European urban farms, and youth exchanges have taken place with a farm in Germany.

Appendix C

SHORT READING LIST

The coming of Post Industrial Society, Daniel Bell, Penguin (1973)

Charities in Britain, Conservatism or Change David Gerard, Bedford Square Press (1983)

Survey of Research on Working Time and Leisure Time, European Foundation (1983)

Which Work Ought to be Paid, Volonteurope Journal No.5

Organising Voluntary Agencies, Margaret Harris, David Billis, Bedford Square Press, (1985)

Voluntary Work and Unemployment in four European Countries, Policy Studies Institute (1987) Dartington Trust

How Green is Your City, Joan Davidson, Bedford Square Press (1988)

Living Conditions in Urban Areas, European Foundation (1986)

European Communities — Commission

Voluntary Work and the Environment:
Local Environmental Development Initiatives in Europe

Luxembourg: Office for Official Publications of the European Communities

1992 — 100 pp. — 16 × 23.5 cm

ISBN 92-826-3650-X

Price (excluding VAT) in Luxembourg: ECU 10,50

Venta y suscripciones • Salg og abonnement • Verkauf und Abonnement • Πωλήσεις και συνδρομές
Sales and subscriptions • Vente et abonnements • Vendita e abbonamenti
Verkoop en abonnementen • Venda e assinaturas

BELGIQUE / BELGIË

**Moniteur belge /
Belgisch Staatsblad**
Rue de Louvain 42 / Leuvenseweg 42
1000 Bruxelles / 1000 Brussel
Tél. (02) 512 00 26
Fax 511 01 84
CCP / Postrekening 000-2005502-27

Autres distributeurs /
Overige verkooppunten

**Librairie européenne/
Europese Boekhandel**
Avenue Albert Jonnart 50 /
Albert Jonnartlaan 50
1200 Bruxelles / 1200 Brussel
Tél. (02) 734 02 81
Fax 735 08 60

Jean De Lannoy
Avenue du Roi 202 /Koningslaan 202
1060 Bruxelles / 1060 Brussel
Tél. (02) 538 51 69
Télex 63220 UNBOOK B
Fax (02) 538 08 41

CREDOC
Rue de la Montagne 34 / Bergstraat 34
Bte 11 / Bus 11
1000 Bruxelles / 1000 Brussel

DANMARK

**J. H. Schultz Information A/S
EF-Publikationer**
Ottiliavej 18
2500 Valby
Tlf. 36 44 22 66
Fax 36 44 01 41
Girokonto 6 00 08 86

BR DEUTSCHLAND

Bundesanzeiger Verlag
Breite Straße
Postfach 10 80 06
5000 Köln 1
Tel. (02 21) 20 29-0
Telex ANZEIGER BONN 8 882 595
Fax 20 29 278

GREECE/ΕΛΛΑΔΑ

G.C. Eleftheroudakis SA
International Bookstore
Nikis Street 4
10563 Athens
Tel. (01) 322 63 23
Telex 219410 ELEF
Fax 323 98 21

ESPAÑA

Boletín Oficial del Estado
Trafalgar, 27
28010 Madrid
Tel. (91) 44 82 135

Mundi-Prensa Libros, S.A.
Castelló, 37
28001 Madrid
Tel. (91) 431 33 99 (Libros)
431 32 22 (Suscripciones)
435 36 37 (Dirección)
Télex 49370-MPLI-E
Fax (91) 575 39 98

Sucursal:

Librería Internacional AEDOS
Consejo de Ciento, 391
08009 Barcelona
Tel. (93) 301 86 15
Fax (93) 317 01 41

**Llibreria de la Generalitat
de Catalunya**
Rambla dels Estudis, 118 (Palau Moja)
08002 Barcelona
Tel. (93) 302 68 35
302 64 62
Fax (93) 302 12 99

FRANCE

**Journal officiel
Service des publications
des Communautés européennes**
26, rue Desaix
75727 Paris Cedex 15
Tél. (1) 40 58 75 00
Fax (1) 40 58 75 74

IRELAND

Government Supplies Agency
4-5 Harcourt Road
Dublin 2
Tel. (1) 61 31 11
Fax (1) 78 06 45

ITALIA

Licosa Spa
Via Duca di Calabria, 1/1
Casella postale 552
50125 Firenze
Tel. (055) 64 54 15
Fax 64 12 57
Telex 570466 LICOSA I
CCP 343 509

GRAND-DUCHÉ DE LUXEMBOURG

Messageries Paul Kraus
11, rue Christophe Plantin
2339 Luxembourg
Tél. 499 88 88
Télex 2515
Fax 499 88 84 44
CCP 49242-63

NEDERLAND

SDU Overheidsinformatie
Externe Fondsen
Postbus 20014
2500 EA 's-Gravenhage
Tel. (070) 37 89 911
Fax (070) 34 75 778

PORTUGAL

Imprensa Nacional
Casa da Moeda, EP
Rua D. Francisco Manuel de Melo, 5
1092 Lisboa Codex
Tel. (01) 69 34 14

**Distribuidora de Livros
Bertrand, Ld.ª**
Grupo Bertrand, SA
Rua das Terras dos Vales, 4-A
Apartado 37
2700 Amadora Codex
Tel. (01) 49 59 050
Telex 15798 BERDIS
Fax 49 60 255

UNITED KINGDOM

HMSO Books (PC 16)
HMSO Publications Centre
51 Nine Elms Lane
London SW8 5DR
Tel. (071) 873 2000
Fax GP3 873 8463
Telex 29 71 138

ÖSTERREICH

**Manz'sche Verlags-
und Universitätsbuchhandlung**
Kohlmarkt 16
1014 Wien
Tel. (0222) 531 61-0
Telex 11 25 00 BOX A
Fax (0222) 531 61-39

SUOMI

Akateeminen Kirjakauppa
Keskuskatu 1
PO Box 128
00101 Helsinki
Tel. (0) 121 41
Fax (0) 121 44 41

NORGE

Narvesen information center
Bertrand Narvesens vei 2
PO Box 6125 Etterstad
0602 Oslo 6
Tel. (2) 57 33 00
Telex 79668 NIC N
Fax (2) 68 19 01

SVERIGE

BTJ
Box 200
22100 Lund
Tel. (046) 18 00 00
Fax (046) 18 01 25

SCHWEIZ / SUISSE / SVIZZERA

OSEC
Stampfenbachstraße 85
8035 Zürich
Tel. (01) 365 54 49
Fax (01) 365 54 11

CESKOSLOVENSKO

NIS
Havelkova 22
13000 Praha 3
Tel. (02) 235 84 46
Fax 42-2-264775

MAGYARORSZÁG

Euro-Info-Service
Budapest I. Kir.
Attila út 93
1012 Budapest
Tel. (1) 56 82 11
Telex (22) 4717 AGINF H-61
Fax (1) 17 59 031

POLSKA

Business Foundation
ul. Krucza 38/42
00-512 Warszawa
Tel. (22) 21 99 93, 628-28-82
International Fax&Phone
(0-39) 12-00-77

JUGOSLAVIJA

Privredni Vjesnik
Bulevar Lenjina 171/XIV
11070 Beograd
Tel. (11) 123 23 40

CYPRUS

**Cyprus Chamber of Commerce and
Industry**
Chamber Building
38 Grivas Dhigenis Ave
3 Deligiorgis Street
PO Box 1455
Nicosia
Tel. (2) 449500/462312
Fax (2) 458630

TÜRKIYE

**Pres Gazete Kitap Dergi
Pazarlama Dağitim Ticaret ve sanayi
AŞ**
Narlibahçe Sokak N. 15
Istanbul-Cağaloğlu
Tel. (1) 520 92 96 - 528 55 66
Fax 520 64 57
Telex 23822 DSVO-TR

CANADA

Renouf Publishing Co. Ltd
Mail orders — Head Office:
1294 Algoma Road
Ottawa, Ontario K1B 3W8
Tel. (613) 741 43 33
Fax (613) 741 54 39
Telex 0534783

Ottawa Store:
61 Sparks Street
Tel. (613) 238 89 85

Toronto Store:
211 Yonge Street
Tel. (416) 363 31 71

UNITED STATES OF AMERICA

UNIPUB
4611-F Assembly Drive
Lanham, MD 20706-4391
Tel. Toll Free (800) 274 4888
Fax (301) 459 0056

AUSTRALIA

Hunter Publications
58A Gipps Street
Collingwood
Victoria 3066

JAPAN

Kinokuniya Company Ltd
17-7 Shinjuku 3-Chome
Shinjuku-ku
Tokyo 160-91
Tel. (03) 3439-0121

Journal Department
PO Box 55 Chitose
Tokyo 156
Tel. (03) 3439-0124

**AUTRES PAYS
OTHER COUNTRIES
ANDERE LÄNDER**

**Office des publications officielles
des Communautés européennes**
2, rue Mercier
2985 Luxembourg
Tél. 49 92 81
Télex PUBOF LU 1324 b
Fax 48 85 73/48 68 17
CC bancaire BIL 8-109/6003/700